RAPID REGENCY

AN AUTHOR'S QUICK GUIDE TO WRITING REGENCY ROMANCE

JEWEL ALLEN

Special thanks to the following: My editor, beta readers, and author friends for the valuable feedback. My a-maize-ing sprinting friends, without whose patience with my corny jokes I wouldn't have been able to get through the never-ending sprints. As always, my husband and children for your love and patience and helping me brainstorm swoony dashing dukes. Last but not the least, my Heavenly Father for giving me the opportunity to create stories.

Thanks to Josi Kilpack and Maggie Dallen who graciously shared their advice in my Q&As. And to British expatriate and author Karen Pierotti (published as Karen M. Edwards) for sharing her perspective from across the pond.

Join my Rapid Releasers Facebook group. Subscribe to my newsletter at www.jewelallen.com/subscribe.

SO YOU WANT TO WRITE A REGENCY ROMANCE

I'M HERE to tell you that you can. Believing in yourself is half the battle.

How do I know? Because I've been in your shoes before.

After rapid releasing a majority of my thirty-plus contemporary and a smattering of non-Regency historical novels over the past three years, I encountered a steep learning curve writing my first Regency romance.

Oh, it wasn't for lack of resources; it was the opposite. I had so many options, I hardly knew where to start. I needed more of a Cliff Notes version to ease me into things; instead, I had a world library at my fingertips.

This is the book I wish I had when I jumped into the genre. Between these pages, I will lay out the process and research that helped me write a 25K word Regency romance novella in five days. It will give you a clearer understanding of the time period, without the overwhelm.

As bonus material, I have included Q&As with Regency romance authors who will share how they started. And how, with courage, hard work and dedication, they are now enjoying success in the genre. One of my British author friends, Karen Pierotti, also graciously allowed me to include her essay, "Thoughts from a Brit."

But first, let me give you a bit of a backstory.

~

Since I started self-publishing novels in 2014, I'd often considered writing a Regency romance. Every time I thought about writing in that genre, however, I got cold feet. To combat my fear, I read numerous books, blogs, and talked to Regency authors, only to end up feeling more over-whelmed and scared.

I was about to shelf my ambition when 2020 rolled around.

At the start of the year, one of my author-publisher friends invited me to write a novella in one of her sweet romance series, a majority of books of which are set in Regency and Victorian England.

At the outset, I wanted to say no. Even though I had been self-publishing since 2014, I was scared to commit to such a daunting goal. I'd mostly written contemporary romance after all. And though I'd written historical romance and knew how to conduct research, I didn't know how to write Regency. Oh, sure, I'd read the genre vora-ciously as a new stay-at-home mom, but that was some two decades ago.

Despite my fears, I took the plunge and signed on. More as a dare to myself.

A dare that kind of broadsided me when 2020 happened.

Apart from my having to write through the turmoil of a global pandemic, my mother fell seriously ill in August and passed away unexpectedly.

Just as my Regency manuscript was almost due.

I'm the type of person, that when I commit, I'm all in. With all the research I needed to do, I didn't think I'd make it. It was a terribly, terribly difficult time, where I could barely function. After a few despairing weeks, I was tempted to contact my publisher and tell her that I simply couldn't do it. I was sure she would have understood.

To my surprise, somehow I pulled through and I was able write my way through grief. I would dare say my writing saved me, allowing me to channel my sorrow and tender feelings into fictional scenes.

Emailing a draft of *Lady Serena's Choice* to my publisher, I knew it was one of the proudest moments of my authorial career. I was able to jump into an unfamiliar genre, get out of my comfort zone during a personally challenging time, and learn a lot in the process.

In case I haven't made it super clear yet, even though I have a journalistic background that spans two decades and I do my due diligence with research, I'm no Regency era expert. Let's get that out of the way.

My guess is that those who write Regency romances have not only done their homework but also have had the guts to write in one of the top-selling genres of romance. As I interviewed Regency romance authors for my weekly author Q&A on my blog, I realized a huge difference setting them apart from aspiring Regency romance writers like me and you is that they overcame their self-doubts and jumped into a perennial reader favorite that has stood the test of time. Kudos to these authors who *have* put in the research in a genre with more-than-your-average-discerning reviewers, which I am sure helped them go forward with self-confidence.

How hot is the genre? Regency authors from the get-go can make serious money (some earn $5,000 their first month, especially with the right networking) without advertising. Makes sense. After all, we are talking about a genre of romance set in one of the most memorable time periods in the United Kingdom that has unleashed a whole sub-genre in itself.

For many aspiring Regency authors like myself, who have never set foot on British soil nor know the cadence of British speech (apart from our exposure to Hollywood), fear is enough to keep us from trying. Due to self-elimination, many quit before even starting / trying, therefore the number of authors working to meet the demands of a voracious readership aren't what they could / should be. I was one such reader myself. As a new mom some two decades ago, once I discovered Regency, I read *everything* I could get my hands on in that section of the library.

My goal is to keep this book fairly basic so as not to overwhelm you. When I started my journey it was like drinking through a fire hose! I would like to give you building blocks instead. I hope that after reading *Rapid Regency* and referring to it often, you will have a good foundation you can confidently build on for years to come.

What this book isn't: it will not teach you the basics of self-publishing nor the craft of writing. There are lots of other books dedicated to those topics.

~

Let me explain how this book is organized. Each chapter topic is sequential in nature, based generally on my own process as a novelist, and specifically on my experience as a researcher while writing my first Regency romance.

This was my mental thread: "What is the Regency period? What social classes do my main characters belong to and where will my story be set? What is the landscape in my fictional setting?" And so on.

My goal is to give you enough information on each topic so you can start brainstorming, outlining, and writing your Regency novel today. Feel free to read through the book completely and then jump around as your research requires.

My sources and other recommended resources will be listed at the end of some chapters and at the end of the book. Should you want to, you can look up topics as you have time or interest.

2

WHAT WAS THE REGENCY ERA, ANYWAY?

FOR SUCH A SHORT time span—nine years from 1811 to 1820—in British history, the Regency Era left its astounding mark on the world.

Jennifer Kloester, author of *Georgette Heyer's Regency World,* as well as authors of other Regency references, acknowledge that the term Greater Regency has loosely been applied to the years 1780 through 1830. This is due to the fact that George IV influenced many aspects of this European nation during those decades.

It is important to note, however, that the years prior to 1811 are considered "Georgian," and the years after 1820 "Victorian." Those years between Regency and Victorian are technically Georgian but there's a lot of debate between historians about what to call them.

For the bulk of this book, I will focus on the True Regency—the years of 1811 to 1820.

Who was the Prince Regent?

On February 5, 1811, the British parliament appointed George, Prince of Wales, as Prince Regent (thus the name Regency). Four months before that, in November 1810, his father, King George III, descended into insanity. Soon afterward, Prince George became regent under the terms of the Regency Act of 1811. "Prinny" was 48.

As the eldest child born to King George III and Charlotte Sophia of Mecklenburg-Strelitz on August 12, 1762, Prince George led a flamboyant life. By the time he was a teenager, he exhibited a fondness for the high life. At 17, he already had a reputation for women and wine.

Five years later, at 22, he met the love of his life, Maria Fitzherbert. Theirs was a romance that Regency scandals are made of. Six years his senior and twice widowed, the wealthy Mrs. Fitzherbert became a prominent figure in London society before catching the eye of the young prince. However, they couldn't marry. First, she was Roman Catholic and second, he was under the age of 25 and he couldn't marry without the king's consent.

Yet they secretly married on December 15, 1785. A decade later, the prince abandoned her to marry his Brunswick cousin Princess Caroline. This calculated move induced Parliament to pay his debts. A legal marriage (this time) didn't stop him from carrying on dalliances with other women. After the birth of their only child, Princess Charlotte (1796-1817), the couple separated. Upon George IV's accession to the throne in 1820, Caroline tried to claim her rights as queen consort but the House of Lords vigorously tried to deny her rights. Eventually her death in 1821 made it a moot point.

War formed a backdrop to this extraordinary age of culture and excess--of wealth amidst poverty in a deeply stratified class system.

If Regency society seemed quick to forgive George IV for his shortcomings, it may have been largely because he was an astute and generous patron of the arts. Under his patronage, architect John Nash designed Regent Street and Regent's Park in London. Windsor Castle underwent restoration. His most famous legacy was the Nash-designed Royal Pavilion at Brighton with its exotic Indian and Chinese motif.

With his dissolute lifestyle, he encountered health issues related to his obesity. He died at the age of 68 in the early hours of June 6, 1830. Autopsy results showed he suffered from a ruptured stomach blood vessel, a large bladder tumor the size of an orange, and an enlarged heart.

Despite his departure from this life criticized as one of the least effective monarchs in British history, he got the last laugh. His memory is now associated with what is arguably one of the most glittering and interesting periods in world history.

ON RESEARCH AND LANGUAGE

For an earlier published historical series set in 1780s Spain and the Philippines, I conducted two to three years of research.

In contrast, due to my other book deadlines, I ended up with roughly a month to research and draft my first Regency romance. There were days when I was forced to research and write, despite the challenging circumstances. Luckily, I was able to complete my first draft within my deadline.

I started my research with the low hanging fruit of Wikipedia, just to see what sources were available and to understand the scope of my topic. Since Wikipedia is crowd-sourced with sometimes uncited sources, I always double-check the references in the footnotes and cross-reference facts with a subscription site like Britannica. I poked around to see if I could access primary sources, and to learn what blogs had to say about the topic. Sometimes information would contradict each other, more often times not. When in doubt, I asked in the Facebook historical groups I belong to, where more experienced writers generously shared their knowledge.

I will never try to knowingly distort historical accuracy, but I also allow myself to take creative license if it helps the plot or characterization. With any fiction book, really. I probably do this the most regarding the strictures on women in history. If they just sat home and embroidered all day, I would think it would make for a dull story. When I deviate from what might be more "accurate," I would add an author's note explaining why.

As a last bastion of accuracy, I hired a knowledgeable editor (who was well-versed in the Regency era) to check my manuscripts, both fiction and non-fiction.

Before we plunge into the rest of the book, let me share some advice that applies not only in this genre but to publishing in general.

Some readers just want a good story and might not care so much about historical accuracy. Some will flay you over mistakes, as we are all apt to make, regardless of how much research you conduct. I have heard of Regency readers being overly particular and who wouldn't hesitate to scold an author.

Correct your mistakes and learn from them, square your shoulders, and keep going. With each story you write, you'll only improve.

As for language, write in whichever way feels naturally to you. If you are steeped in Regency romances, your writing/work will probably resemble Jane Austen's. If you'd rather be clear in your storytelling to the modern reader than use Regency slang heavily, that is perfectly fine too.

Just be careful to not use words that wouldn't have been invented then, as well as Americanisms.

A good editor well-versed in the era can be your ally as you polish your manuscript. When it's all said and done, however, the responsibility for accuracy falls on the shoulders of the author, so make sure you do your research to the best of your ability.

On a final note, I have noticed that the Regency romances I enjoy the most have beautiful language and a good sense of place, with a dream-like quality about them. I know of a Regency author who reads poetry to get herself in that historical fiction mood. At any rate, emulate the style of the books you enjoy.

REGENCY ROMANCE TROPES

TROPES ARE a great way to signal to a reader what kind of romance they are reading. There's a reason tropes are popular—readers like to read variations of the same narratives. Familiar, but different. On the flipside, using tropes means your story can easily descend into cliché. Freshen it up with a plot twist, use two to three distinct tropes in a story, and you will have a memorable winner.

For my book *Lady Serena's Choice*, I decided to use the forbidden love, class gap and childhood friend romance tropes.

Here are some of the most common ones in Regency romances.

List of Regency Romance Tropes

Amnesia – He or she loses her memory. They are strangers where the one cares for the other. They fall in love, only for the victim's memory to return—and complications from their former lives come crashing down to threaten their love.

Arranged Marriage – They're being married against their will to a stranger or someone they've known they would marry someday. But now they've had a moment to settle into marriagehood, their spouse is starting to look more desirable to them.

Beauty & the Beast – Typically a hero who has physical or emotional scars, shutting out the rest of the world. Until the day the heroine enters his life and is forced to work or live with him under the same roof. She has to overcome her initial aversion for him.

Bluestocking – She is well-read and participates in meetings for progressive-minded women. She can't be bothered with something as silly as love. He's her intellectual match and doesn't talk down to her . . . refreshing traits she finds highly irresistible.

Childhood Friend Romance – They grew up together, when life was sweeter and more innocent. This could easily incorporate forbidden love, where they cannot be together due to their belonging to different classes. Their long history means they know the other person's true self, and how changed their adult self is.

.   .   .

Christmas – They kiss under a mistletoe, they skate on a frozen pond, they return to their small village and enjoy old traditions. How can a yuletide romance not blossom in that setting?

Compromised – By virtue / means of her own actions or not, the heroine's reputation is at stake. The hero steps in to try to save her and salvage what's left of her reputation by proposing marriage. She has no choice but to accept his offer.

Con artist / ruffian – He or she has a secret to hide. It was all about conning other people but now they are starting to care for someone else. Related to *lovable rogue*.

Disability – He or she, or a secondary character, has a disability around which the plot revolves. Related to *patient / caregiver* trope.

Dukes/ Titled Hero – A titled hero is always appealing. After the prince, dukes hold the next powerful title. As the billionaire of the Regency era, the duke easily gets what he wants, except for the heroine's love. She'll make him work hard for it, and he'll fall line, hook and sinker. Earls, Marquesses and Viscounts aren't too far behind in their appeal.

Employer/Employee – They work together, which brings

them closer to each other, but they cannot act on their feelings as it could cause a scandal.

Enemies to Lovers – Their relationship starts off with sparks—the antagonistic kind. They are on opposing sides of an issue, or the other is an obstacle to their goal. The fun part is watching them fight off their attraction to each other.

Estranged lovers reunited – They were in love but their relationship didn't work out, and now their paths cross again. The attraction is still there, shadowed by their reluctance to open their hearts to potential heartbreak once again.

Friends to Lovers – They start out as friends, and then something happens to spark their interest. But they don't dare jeopardize their friendship by jumping into a romance.

Ghost / Guardian angel – An otherworldly spirit plays matchmaker.

Governess – She works for him as a governess to an often adorable child or children. The situation forces them into close proximity along with several opportunities for him to show his sweet side as he interacts with the children. What woman could resist that? The two fall in love but they cannot act on their affection without risking scandal. He is her employer, after all, and although she isn't exactly a servant, she isn't his equal either.

Heroes with professions – Physicians, barristers, professors and other educated heroes, who do not perform manual labor, fall under this category. The hero often belongs to a gentry family that possesses great wealth and large estates.

House Party – Singles are thrown together in a house party, often taking place in the country with lots of horse riding and activities to entertain the guests . . . a sure recipe for romance.

India / Far-flung lands – The British Crown traded and colonized other countries, India being one of them. A romance in a lush, exotic setting? Yes, please.

Inventor – The Regency era and beyond was a time of cultural and scientific progress. The hero or heroine could be involved with any of the sciences, more intent on their experiments than the opposite sex. Until they meet each other and suddenly a person is the object of their fascination.

Kidnapping – To avoid descending into a Stockholm syndrome situation, where the hostage falls in love with their captor in kind of an unhealthy way, the victim could have been kidnapped due to mistaken identity. Related to *lovable rogue.*

Loveable Rogue – The hero is just plain trouble. Still, the heroine can't help but fall in love with him. Especially when he starts showing redeemable characteristics. He could fleece the heroine, but instead, he gives up his own comforts for her. He hardly has food in the pantry, and yet gives his last bite to a stray dog.

Marriage and Inheritance – They need to marry to inherit a sizable amount of money. So they do – and find love in the bargain.

Marriage of Convenience – Getting married is mutually beneficial, but they make a pact that no feelings will be involved, until there are.

Masquerade – They meet each other masked and fall in love, but they part before they could determine the other's identity. Related to *secret/hidden identity.*

Mistaken Identity – They mistake the other for someone else, or they are trying to hide their identity. When they fall in love, will coming clean drive the other away?

Patient/Caretaker Heroine – He is the grumpy, uncooperative patient and she is the (un)lucky nurse assigned to help him along.

Protector – She's a waif needing protection from ruffians or villains. But watch out, she's got a spine, and resents his intervention while fighting her attraction to him.

Rags to Riches – He or she starts out poor in the story and then rises to wealth. If it is the hero, he is now able to court the heroine, but there is a lingering bias against him from her family because of his background.

Rake – He has a reputation, deserved or not, for being a skirt-chaser and finally meets his match in the virginal heroine who refuses to succumb to his charms.

Road Trip / Runaway – He and she are forced to travel together over a period of days with the same shared mission, or she's running away and he keeps her company. Because of the close proximity, they can't help but fall in love. But they know this can't last forever; eventually, they will have to part ways, so they fight their feelings.

Secret-agent – He or she is a spy for the government, but must keep their identity secret. They must not get too close, or the secret will get out, which could have deadly consequences. Related to the *Agents of the Crown* trope.

· · ·

Scandal – Pursuing their relationship can lead to the biggest scandal, and they will have to choose if their love is worth risking it. Another variation is, one or the other is embroiled in a scandal and they have to overcome the resulting prejudices.

Seafaring – The 19th century was rife with sea exploration. This is a variation of the road trip. Stowaways and cast-aways can also be part of this trope.

Soldier – He was injured in a battle and returned scarred—physically and/or emotionally. She tries to break down his defenses and he tries to thwart her attempts.

Social class gap – She's the daughter of a titled peer and he's from the working class, or vice versa. If he had prospects—he's working on making himself prosperous, for example—their romance will seem more believable.

Smuggling – A smuggler appears dashing to the heroine, especially when he is trying to steal from the country's enemy.

Spinsters – She's on the shelf, no longer expects marriage, and is perfectly content. The hero must convince her to give up her independence and share a life with him.

· · ·

Ugly Duckling / Beautiful Swan – She starts out plain and grows up to be a ravishing beauty, usually at her coming out or for an occasion. Just as the hero does, everyone takes notice. She attracts a lot of suitors which makes him jealous. The hero has to work doubly hard to win her love, but often she secretly loves him already.

Vicar – He's the staid vicar who must now find a wife. She sees past his stuffy exterior to his generous heart. It's a match made in heaven.

Wager/bet – The hero or heroine makes a wager that they can make the other fall in love with them. As they attempt this, they fall in love in the process. But do they dare reveal their initial prank and risk their relationship?

Widows/Widowers – He or she has lost their spouse and it's hard for them to open their heart once again to love.

BEFORE YOU WRITE: COVER YOUR STORY

ONE OF THE challenges I discovered as I jumped into this genre is finding a quality Regency romance cover where the stock model does not appear already on so many other books. Finding a good, inexpensive cover artist when you are starting out is also difficult though not impossible. (I am actually seeing this situation improve.)

Take a little bit of time before you finalize your story plot to scout around for a cover artist. In general, it is easier to write your story to match the cover than it is the other way around.

I learned this the hard way. For my first Regency, I wanted to have a horse on the cover with the heroine because the spin-off series is horse-themed . . . only to find out that Regency models with horses are hard, if not impossible, to come by. So I ended up picking a photo of a modern bride and hired an author artist to put a bonnet on her.

Here are some of the common ways you can get an affordable cover while still having your books stand out (in a good way).

∾

Commission a custom cover. Ask among Regency authors and you will find cover artists who are on the higher end of custom covers but are still affordable. In the fall of 2020 I was finding a range of $30 (Fiverr) to $300 and upwards for custom covers. A good way to find good artists is to pay attention to covers you like. Click for a sample to find the artist information on the copyright page. If it doesn't name the artist, ask the author.

Pros: You can get the exact look that you want for your cover and can usually face / head swap to match your character. Your cover will have a better chance standing out because it's customized for you while still following genre expectations. If your artist has an established reputation in this genre, that professional will know what kinds of books are selling and can make sure your cover is marketable. Photo manipulation could be pricey, however, and my advice to the aspiring author is to avoid paying premium for covers. Commission the covers you can now and step up as your finances allow.

Trends easily change over the years. For example, studio-like portraits of women in ballgowns have given way to a softer, dreamier outdoorsy look, with the heroine often-times having her back turned to the camera. No doubt the trend will change up and cycle through again. The best way to stay on top of what covers are selling is to google best-selling Regency romances and note what sets their covers apart.

Cons: Some of the higher end artists are pricier especially for the newbie Regency author, and they are booked solid for months. Although your hope is to recoup your cover cost from higher sales (because of the cover) it is not a guarantee. You will also need to invest time as you communicate back and forth with your designer.

I know authors who hire less expensive artists on Fiverr and give them photos from their own custom shoots. There are plenty of talented and reliable Fiverr artists, alongside ones where you get what you pay for. Be sure to ask for sample work and references. Fortunately, Fiverr is usually good at refunding if you are not fully satisfied, but by then you'd have spent a lot of time and anxiety. And still not end up with a good cover. So use Fiverr with caution.

Commission a photo shoot. Authors with a talent for photography can do a photo shoot. These photos can then be given to an artist for use in a custom cover. I have never done this before, but a custom shoot sounds like so much fun.

To save on costs, many authors ask for volunteer models among their friends and family. They will either borrow, buy, or make Regency costumes for the models to wear. Whether or not the model is paid, you will want a signed model release on file.

Buy a premade cover. This blends the best of both worlds: the expertise of a good cover artist with a cover usually a third of their going rate, without the wait. A premade could even inspire a story. Not only are they economical, anywhere from $30 to $100, but they are ready for you *now* and with the least amount of work on your part.

Most reputable Regency cover artists are usually booked for months and their custom covers deservedly are more expensive. One way to benefit from their expertise without the custom cover cost is to stalk their pre-made cover groups on social media.

Occupational hazard warning: It is way too easy to impulse-buy covers. I have so many, it's not even funny, just waiting for that time when I will be inspired to use them. You don't want to dither too long on a good cover if you see one. But don't keep buying covers unless you know for sure that you can use them sometime soon.

Make your own cover. It *is* possible to make a cover if you have a good photo manipulation program and artistic ability. Some established Regency authors orchestrate their own custom photo shoots with relatives, friends, or paid models. However, I would caution you against making your own cover unless you know what you're doing. Typography, for one, can make or break a cover. A homemade looking cover might drive your potential reader to cringe rather than one-click.

One way to make sure you are on the right track is to study bestselling covers. Once you have created your cover, get feedback from cover critique groups or Regency author groups. Details such as hair and dress need to be on point to resonate positively with readers. Usually, getting feedback on my attempts at covers is enough to send me scrambling to hire someone.

Bottomline: Recognize your limitations, and turn it over to the pros if needed.

Do you have to come up with a cover before even typing a single word of your story? It's not a must-do, but based on my experience, I think it's a good idea.

On the flip-side, to some authors, trying to write to a cover when you don't have a good grasp of your story is akin to putting the cart before the horse. If you decide to wait to get the cover until after you draft your story, make sure you plan ahead to get a cover scheduled as good artists book months in advance.

Even if you hire someone else to do your cover, you should already have some stock photos in mind; searching for them tends to be the most time-consuming part.

Whether you are hiring someone or not, here are some sources for Regency stock photos. They vary in prices so be sure to check the fine print for pricing and licenses before buying an image.

Stitch Stock

Period Images

Deposit Photos

Shutterstock

The Killion Group Images

The Reed Files

As you pore over stock photos for your Regency romance, you will want to pay attention to the period-appropriateness of the models' clothing. Be sure to read the chapters on Female and Male Fashion for guidance.

PLANNING A SERIES

Romance readers, including those who love Regency, love series. Large families and a neighborhood full of potential love matches have been featured in a series of books by bestselling authors to much success.

Series are great for the prolific writer for the following reasons:

- If a reader enjoys a book, they will binge-read the rest of the series.
- A series with interesting and recurring characters makes your reader invested in their lives.
- Once a world or shared setting is established, it is easier to write stories featuring the same characters and landmarks. Seeing familiar, lovable people is so fun.

When brainstorming a series, open up the possibility of

future story lines by introducing several secondary characters with multiple plot lines. For example, for a story set in a ducal estate, you could introduce neighboring families. That same estate would rely upon their village for their needs, just as a village would rely on the estate for employment. Adding interesting village characters would make sense. (Think of the opening scene in the animated *Beauty and the Beast*).

As I planned out my first Regency book, I conjured up the next generation of characters—children of the first book's couple. I guess I wasn't too far off the mark when I saw a bestselling author crafting an intergenerational family tree, which she offered to her readers, much to their excitement.

The challenge with writing a series is producing quality stories quickly enough. I won't go into detail about writing quickly because I already cover techniques in my book *Rapid Release*, but here are three ways you can do so in a research-heavy genre like Regency.

1. Stockpile manuscripts. Schedule your books months in advance and write one to two books ahead. This will require discipline and a careful tracking of your wordcount and schedule.

2. Collaborate on a series with other authors. Not only can you capture an eager readership through the rapid publishing schedule, you are also harnessing the combined marketing power of a group of authors.

It is important to choose your collaborators carefully. They don't all have to be the same level of being established, but you should at least admire their writing style because they will impact your author reputation by association. A great collaboration could also yield creative series ideas and a sounding board for your plotline. On the flipside, collaborations can take away from your own books, so choose wisely.

3. Write shorter manuscripts, in the range of 25,000 to 40,000 words. To manage reader expectations, especially to readers who actually prefer longer works of historical fiction (upwards of 50,000 words) you will want to disclose somewhere in the blurb that it is novella-length. Novellas can be fun, smaller story bites. I would encourage you to go for the upper range of book length, though, say 40,000 to 50,000 words. This not only gives your readers more value, but you will earn more from people reading a higher number of pages if you enroll your book in Kindle Unlimited.

As I have written over 24 books in two years in several series, I have learned a few tricks on writing series with good read-through.

Biggest mistake: Having a shared theme but not having the characters move over from the first book to the next. One of my series has the characters popping in and out, or a side couple has their own story, but not in a linear way from book to book. I have featured side characters that aren't family nor close friends and readers don't have as much loyalty to them.

Best moves: Writing a series that has built in read-through, like brothers, or firefighters (alternatively in Regency, having characters be part of a group with shared interests). Adding families and neighbors. Readers *love* families, neighbors and interactions. Having a series-long question on each character that will have their own book someday and stringing it along until they get their own book. And then finally answering that question.

Here are examples of how to set up a series-long question, albeit in contemporary settings.

I have a royal series of brothers. The last one does not even appear in any of the earlier books and I am about ready to tackle his story in a pre-Christmas book. I labeled him as a "black sheep" because he *never* comes home for Christmas but no one knows why. The other characters always mention him though, so he stays in readers' minds. I have had reviews speculate about him. I am excited to do the final reveal.

In a firefighter series, I introduced a misfit side character who is always on the brink of getting fired in all the books. I wrote what could have been a last series book, but instead I wrote him into a redemption first book in a spinoff series.

How is this applicable to the Regency era? Well, obviously, you could still have brothers, or sisters, or friends who share the same interests. You could have side characters with quirks that rise to villainy or heroism, the perfect candidates for the next books in the series.

What is the magic series number? It might differ across the board, but for me I start out with three, then six, and so on. Ideally, I arrange to get the covers done ahead so that there is design continuity and so I can keep putting books out when I'm ready.

You can plan out a six-book series with a re-check midway through to give yourself an exit strategy in case you lose interest or life demands a discontinuation. It is also nice to have boxsets in increments of three. Save yourself having to go back and re-read your stories by setting up a series bible—notes on each book and character, including their quirks and even details like eye color. It also helps to get the same editor or beta reader to check your manuscripts for continuity. If you develop enough of a following, you will end up with eagle-eye readers who will volunteer the corrections. When they do, thank them graciously.

Remember, you do not need to write a series if you do not wish to commit to one. Maybe you are an author who likes the variety of standalones and are ready to move on to a different setting after every book. However, if you set up your world to allow for series, you're giving yourself that option later on.

Writing series requires a fair amount of faith that readers (and you as an author) will stay invested in the world you are building. However, as I've noticed in reviews of books that hit the bestseller lists, readers easily get invested in a family and neighborhood, so it's a gamble that would most likely pay off.

7

GETTING INTO THE REGENCY MOOD

No MATTER how much reading and research you do, you may never feel completely ready to write your first Regency romance. Or your second. Or your third. Or you might be comfortable writing the story, but nervous about self-publishing. Or both. Either way, it can be nerve-wracking.

There I was in the fall of 2020, branching out from contemporary fiction, to write "British lingo" from the 19th century. You bet I was scared. So what did I do? I came up with all sorts of excuses to not write because I was so nervous. Luckily, all the tactics I employed to procrastinate actually helped me finally feel ready.

Here were some of the things I did:

- Watched *Pride & Prejudice*, the 2005 version with Kiera Knightley. This helped re-familiarize me with Regency speech and the conventions of the genre. I know of authors who find it helpful to watch BBC versions of Jane Austen stories as they get the speech patterns just right.
- Watched *Pride & Prejudice & Zombies*. Yes,

really. Although some details were not authentic to the period (the zombies, for starters), the tongue-and-cheek movie captured speech and manners perfectly. Even the weapons were spot-on as far as I could tell. Who knew that Regency moors and forest made for great zombie cover? The romance was swoony and I laughed a lot. And those debutante fight scenes were the bomb! Bonus: my husband, who sat bewildered through the 2005 P&P, actually enjoyed this movie.

- Listened to the free audio version of Jane Austen's *Pride & Prejudice* on YouTube. The recording took roughly 12 hours, so I listened to sections while on a brisk walk, or doing chores around the house, or driving somewhere. Observant Jane Austen was the master of satire. I learned a lot about Regency customs and hierarchy. And she had a wicked sense of humor. Listening to the language of the era also inspired my writing.
- Read bestselling Regency books once or twice for a couple of weeks.
- Studied blurbs of bestselling Regency books to get ideas for tropes and other elements to add to my storylines.
- Read reviews of bestselling Regency books and paid attention to polls in Facebook reader groups to see what readers love (and didn't love).
- Looked up and cooked up recipes of British food from the Regency era. My favorite was crumpets (incidentally, in *Lady Serena's Choice,*

Crumpet is the name of the heroine's horse) except they took hours to rise (twice) and cook in a cast iron skillet on the stove. But they were yummy! British food isn't very colorful and is rather heavy on carbs, but it's hearty and pure comfort.

- Listened to 19th century music.
- Reminded myself that I have watched and read enough Regency stories that when push came to shove, I would remember how people sounded. (I did!)
- Resisted the eye-roll. Even though many things about the Regency period grated on my nerves, such as the social class snobbery and the strictures on women, to name a few, immersing myself in well-written romances reminded me of why I enjoyed them when I was a new mom.

I still had the nerves, but getting myself in the right frame of mind helped. It was time to act. Ready or not, I finally plunged in.

8

NAMING YOUR CHARACTERS

Your Regency story needs to be populated with characters whose names could fit into the time period. For this list of names, I used the 1841 England and Wales Census on Family Search as reference. I looked up Norfolk as I have family there. Simple names seemed to rule the day. Some of the most popular female names were Mary and Elizabeth. John was a popular male name. Biblical names may have been uncommon as the English upper-class did not use them as much as their American counterparts. The census may also have reflected more diversity—including Irish, Scots and Welsh.

Another good source for inspiration is to flip through British estate names and pick a name that rolls nicely off your tongue or fits your characters' personalities.

Naming tip: Try to pick names that don't start with the same letter to avoid confusion. Search for names online for English estates and peers and either use those names or tweak it a little so it's fictional.

True confession: my first Regency heroine's name is Serena Clarke. I learned belatedly that she is a modern-day actress. So I suggest you google your main characters' names first.

Female Names

Agnes
Ann/e
Betsy
Caroline
Catherine
Charlotte
Ellen
Elinor
Elizabeth
Ellen
Emily
Emma
Esther
Georgiana
Hannah
Harriet
Henrietta
Jane
Julia
Letitia
Louisa
Lucia
Margaret
Maria
Martha
Mary

Nancy
Rebecca
Rhoda
Sarah
Sophia
Susanna

Male Names

Augustus
Charles
Edward
Frederick
George
Henry
Herbert
Jeremy
John
Luke
Samuel
Richard
Robert
Stephen
Theophilus
Thomas
William

Surnames

Amies
Browning
Bunting
Cartwright

Cliffe
Dumbrill
Foster
Francis
Gough
Graves
Harper
Highgate
Jacob
Maidment
Moss
Poll
Riddall
Studd
Swann
Taylor
Thompson
Walker
Waters
Watson
Wayman

Actual Dukedoms in Modern Day England
(You can avoid using an actual dukedom name if that is not
your intent, or use it as inspiration as you name your
fictional one.)

Lancaster
Edinburgh
Cornwall
Cambridge
Sussex

York
Gloucester
Kent
Beaufort
Bedford
Devonshire
Grafton
Brandon
Manchester
Norfolk
Northumberland
Richmond
Gordon
Rutland
Somerset
St Albans
Sutherland
Wellington

9

HISTORICAL EVENTS

FICTIONAL CHARACTERS' lives seldom unfold in a vacuum, unless they end up shipwrecked on an uninhabited island. Because I wanted to write a novel with a next-generation sequel (featuring the first book heroine's daughter), I chose to set my story in 1800. That way, book two's heroine would be of marriageable age in 1820.

When trying to establish a time frame for your Regency romance, it pays off to look at the date in context of historical events. Doing so could add sub-plots that will enrich your story and give your character actions and decisions context and an interesting backdrop. If you are starting out, I would keep to the era's official years since earlier or later years would require more research and possibly have different genre expectations. Make sure to look up historical events during your story's timeline to add depth and context. Let history be a prompt to all those stories you can write someday.

George Augustus Frederick, Prince of Wales, began his nine-year tenure as regent and became known as The Prince Regent. He held a fete at 9:00 p.m. June 19, 1811, at Carlton House in celebration of his assumption of the Regency.

This sub-period of the Georgian era began the formal Regency.

1812

Shipping and territory disputes started the War of 1812 between the United Kingdom and the United States. Tensions between the two countries already were heightened from the French revolutionary (1792-99) and Napoleonic Wars (1799-1815). Nearly three years later in 1815, the war concluded with the Treaty of Ghent.

1813

Pride and Prejudice by "a lady" (Jane Austen, anonymously writing as the same author of *Sense and Sensibility*) was published.

1814

Allies invaded France, leading to the Treaty of Paris.

Napoleon abdicated and was exiled to Elba, a Mediterranean island off the coast of Tuscany, Italy.

This was the last time the River Thames froze, and the last time the River Thames Frost Fair was held.

Gas lighting was introduced in London streets.

. . .

1815

Napoleon I of France defeated at the Battle of Water-loo. He was exiled to St. Helena.

The British Crown invaded and annexed Kingdom of Kandy (an independent monarchy of the island of Sri Lanka).

1816

Mount Tambora, a volcano on the island of Sumbawa, Indonesia, erupts. Europe, still recovering from the Napoleonic Wars, suffered from food shortages. A "year without a summer" was an especially difficult time for the poor. Low temperatures and heavy rains resulted in failed harvests in Britain. Hungry people demonstrated in front of grain markets and bakeries. Later, riots, arson and looting took place in many European cities. Beau Brummell, hounded by creditors, fled to France.

1817

Antonin Carême, a French chef and an early practitioner and exponent of the elaborate style of cooking known as *grande cuisine*, created a spectacular feast for the Prince Regent at the Royal Pavilion in Brighton.

1818

Piccadilly Circus constructed in London. *Frankenstein* published.

1819

Princess Alexandrina Victoria (future Queen Victoria) was christened in Kensington Palace.

Ivanhoe by Walter Scott was published.

Sir Stamford Raffles, a British administrator, founded Singapore.

First steam-propelled vessel (the SS Savannah) crossed the Atlantic and arrived in Liverpool from Savannah, Georgia.

1820

Death of George III and accession of The Prince Regent as George IV. Royal Astronomical Society founded.

10

BRITISH COUNTIES OF REGENCY ENGLAND

As a Regency romance writer, you can either make up a setting for your story or use a real location. The advantage with the first is that you would have the freedom to make up names and details without having to stay true to actual names and landmarks, especially if you are not familiar with England.

With the second, if done with careful research, you can recreate a Regency setting that will ring true with your readers, enriched with details you don't have to make up. In fact, sometimes, a particular setting grows on you. Be sure to save your research so you can refer to it time and time again. Maybe you have family or friends from a particular location. Wouldn't it be fun to get to know more of that area?

Even if you decide to make up a location for your story, it would be helpful to base it on an actual county or geographical area of England. That way, you can accurately depict the climate and terrain as well as flora and fauna. Another advantage is, when mentioning real places like London, you could peg a specific area on a Regency map and calculate the distance from your fictional location.

For example, in *Lady Serena's Choice*, I had decided I wanted the setting to be by the coast but close enough to Melton (at least on the same parallel), where I wanted to set a fox hunt. I made up a fictitious place name, Derryshire, and set it along the northeast coast. To make my setting more authentic, I looked up plants I would find in that part of England.

The following are British counties listed in the 1841 England and Wales Census. I could have added Wales to the mix, but I decided not to, since Welsh culture would deservedly require more research on its own right.

Each listing has a brief description. May these details spark some story plot ideas whether you fictionalize a place or not. Read blogs or watch YouTube videos to get a better sense of place.

For a good visual map of the different counties, check out an article on Wikimedia, *Historic counties of England*.

Source: 1824 *Gray's Book of Roads*, by George Carrington Gray, in public domain.

Counties and Descriptions

Home Counties

Berkshire – The historic market town of Newbury, and nearby Lambourn are famous for racehorse training. Eton College, a well-known boys' school, is located here. The English royal residence, Windsor Castle, occupies 13 acres above the south bank of the River Thames.

•   •   •

Essex – Low-lying county with a flat coast of tidal inlets and islands. Some tracts of land never converted to farmland survived as woodland, notably Epping Forest. The rich soil produced heavy yields of crops. With the construction of railways in the 19th century, seaside towns of Southend and on the Tendring coast attracted Londoners. Despite its proximity to London, Essex stayed rural.

Middlesex – County of southeastern England includes Central London north of the River Thames and surrounding areas to the north and west. For centuries was the county retreat of royalty and wealthy London merchants. Most notable building is the royal palace of Hampton Court.

Surrey – Forested hills, house hunting preserves (Henry VIII owned a lodge at Nonesuch Park) and a source of timber for charcoal, construction and shipbuilding. The Surrey Iron Railway from Wandsworth to Merstham, which utilized work by horses. It was a public toll railway, providing a track for independent goods hauliers to use their own horses and wagons. It was the first public railway sanctioned by the British Parliament in 1801. The Surrey Iron Railway was commercially successful only briefly, until shortly after the opening of the canal between Croydon and London in 1809. The advent of the steam locomotive spelled the end for horse-drawn railways.

Terrain: lowland crossed by two east-west ridges—one of chalk hills and the other a band of greensand rocks.

· · ·

South

Kent – Also nicknamed "The Garden of England." White Cliffs of Dover, section of coastline facing the Strait of Dover and France. Eight-mile cliff face is chalk accented by streaks of black flint. On a clear day, they are visible from the French coast. Dover Castle is the largest castle in England.

Hampshire - The county town is Winchester, England's capital city until the late 11th century. The county is known as the home of writers Jane Austen and Charles Dickens. Hampshire is also the childhood home of Florence Nightingale. Low, flat lands support heathland and woodland habitats, a large area of which forms part of the New Forest.

Known for its mild climate, coastal scenery, and verdant landscape of fields, Isle of Wight has downland (hills of exposed chalk) and chines (a steep-sided coastal gorge where a river flows to the sea through, typically, soft eroding cliffs of sandstone or clays). There are twenty chines on the Isle of Wight, which has spun fascinating folklore around local smuggling, fishing and shipwrecks.

Sussex – Boasts good-tasting mutton from the marshes. Brighton is best known as a seaside resort. Rye is steeped with history of smuggling and the Hawkhurst Gang. Rye was a favorite place for many authors like American Henry James.

· · ·

Wiltshire – Famous home of the Stone Henge and the Salisbury Cathedral. Also the White Horse, an ancient carving on the low hills in that area, and Avesbury, another Neolithic henge associated with King Arthur.

West Country

Cornwall – Occupying a peninsula in southwestern England, Cornwall is the most remote of English counties. It borders River Tamar to the east, some 200 miles from London. Cornwall's most westernmost town, Penzance, is another 80 miles farther from London and close to Land's End, traditionally considered the southwestern extreme of Great Britain. The inland areas are marked by a series of granite moorlands and drowned river valleys, or rias. Rias, combined with the rocks, produced an attractive coastal landscape.

The sea affects Cornwall's climate. High winds and sea mists blanket the area usually. It rains a lot and often, especially on higher ground. It is warm in the summer and relatively mild in the winter, leading to lush vegetation.

Incidentally, this is the setting of Daphne du Maurier's gothic suspense novel *Rebecca*, published in 1938. Agatha Christie was from Torquay. This county is also associated with King Arthur.

Devon – Forms part of the South West Peninsula of Great Britain. Bounded to the west by Cornwall and to the east by Dorset and Somerset. The economy depends on agriculture and related industries. A quarter of the county is heath or moorland, with rough grazing mainly on Exmoor (setting of the historical novel *Lorna Doone*) and Dartmoor. These areas have wild pony herds called Exmoor and Dartmoor. The coastal areas have picturesque small towns and villages, such as Salcombe, Lynmouth, and Clovelly. Has a lot of steep hills. Winters are mild.

Bristol Channel lies to the north. It abuts the English Channel to the south. Terrain: shallow marshy valleys, thin infertile soils, and coarse grasses, heather and bracken. Climate: generally mild, though temperatures become more extreme with elevation and distance from the sea.

Dorset – A portion of this county was immortalized in the writings of Thomas Hardy, author of *Far from the Madding Crowd* (1874). Chalk uplands cross the terrain.

Gloucestershire – comprises the hilly uplands of the Cotswolds, Forest of Dean, Stroud, the boroughs of Chelthenham and Tewkesbury, and the city of Gloucester. The area has several imposing Norman castles, reflecting the nearness of the Welsh. The Cotswolds' traditional production of sheep and wool into the late 18th century gave way to cattle and farming. In the county's northeastern corner, apple, pear, and plum orchards flourished.

The import of Jamaican sugar and cacao from West Africa led to the creation of the "sugar houses" of Bristol and to chocolate manufacturing. It also is a well-known port. The term "ship shape in Bristol fashion" came from there. NOTE: Though Bristol is listed as a county, in the 1800s it would have been part of Gloucestershire as a major town.

. . .

Somerset – Known for its cider production and the village of Cheddar, the cheese first made there, as well as Bath, its historic spa town, where Jane Austen lived for five years and set two of her novels in.

Midlands

Derbyshire – Situated in the East Midlands of England. The landscape varies from bleak moorlands to lowlands. Largely a pastoral county, with some mining and quarrying, until the 18th century. The first modern factory in England, a silk mill in Derby, was built in 1717. In 1771, the first water-powered cotton-spinning mill was opened at Cromford. The county is richly endowed with great houses dating as far back as the 15th century.

Herefordshire – The gently rolling countryside is more heavily wooded than most of England. The Hereford cattle breed is world famous. Adjoining Greater London to the south.

Leicestershire – This sparsely populated upland hosts some of England's most famous foxhunts. The market town of Melton Mowbray is considered the cradle of foxhunting. Hunting boxes or lodges accommodated the mostly male hunting clientele. From around 1800, the large influx of top-class horses and hard-riding men gave rise to a booming economy of farriers, livery stables, forage suppliers, saddlers, loriners (a maker of small iron objects), and bootmakers.

The county is well-known for its sheep, Stilton cheese, and pork pies. This is a county of country houses rather than of great buildings.

Lincolnshire - Marked by large churches, abbeys, and monasteries, which attest to its agrarian prosperity.

Rutland – Smallest county, historic or otherwise, in England. Has many fine old churches and houses, known for high quality from local sandstone beds. The site of the traditional Cottesmore foxhunt.

Shropshire – This county has a history of Welsh incursions and baronial rebellions.

Staffordshire – The long-established pottery industry in the north became famous during the 1700s, especially through businessman Josiah Wedgwood.

Nottinghamshire – Best known for Sherwood Forest, Robin Hood's turf.

Northamptonshire – Has a large number of mansions and country houses, including the ancestral home of the family of George Washington, the first president of the United States. Noted for great estates and parks, rolling pastoral lands and some of Britain's best-know foxhunts, like the Pytchley.

Warwickshire – County famous for Stratford-upon-Avon, the 16th century birthplace of William Shakespeare.

Worcestershire – Old churches, abbeys, and priories dot the area. And yes, Worcestershire (WUUS-tər-shər) sauce, a fermented liquid condiment, was created in Worcester during the first half of the 19th century.

North

Cheshire – The underlying sandstones and marls give a distinctive red coloring to soils and building stones in churches. During the 18th century, many of Cheshire's towns specialized in textile manufacturing. Some produced silk and others produced cotton. Manchester was a mere market town of 10,000 people in 1717; by 1851 its textile (mainly cotton) industries boomed so much so that the city boasted more than 300,000 residents.

Cumberland– Extreme northwestern England, bounded on the north by Scotland. It lies along the coast, facing Solway Firth and the Irish Sea. The coastal plain rises in the south to the Cumbrian Mountains, reaching 3,210 feet at Scafell

Pike, the highest point in England. At the center of this county is the fertile Vale of Eden.

Durham – Located in northeastern England, on the North Sea coast. The county got the world's first passenger railway, which began operation in 1825. It ran between Stockton and Darlington, turning the latter into a center of locomotive production and railway engineering.

Lancashire – The Industrial Revolution originated in Lancashire during the 18th century with the introduction of cotton manufacturing, along with the use of waterpower, the mechanization of spinning, and the adoption of the factory system.

Northumberland – England's northernmost county. Has varied landscape, from agricultural eastern coastal plain, rugged hills and wild moors. The coast experiences cool sea fogs. In the 1770s at least of Northumberland was still wasteland. Parts of the moors are still among the most sparsely populated areas of England.

Westmorland - Main activity in Westmorland was sheepherding. The Lake poets—William Wordsworth, Samuel Taylor Coleridge, and Robert Southey—popularized the Lake District in the early 1800s. Later merged with Cumberland.

• • •

Yorkshire –Notable among the great 18th-century country houses are Wentworth Woodhouse and Castle Howard. It also has three areas called Ridings.

East of England

Bedfordshire – An area of low, rolling terrain at the headwaters of several river systems. Central Bedfordshire is the home of the majestic Woburn Abbey.

Buckinghamshire – Location of Chiltern Hills or the Chilterns, officially designated as an "Area of Outstanding Natural Beauty." The Chilterns encompasses Buckinghamshire, Oxfordshire, Hertfordshire and Bedfordshire. Overlooks the Vale of Aylesbury. Terrain: countryside, beech woodland. During Regency times, this county was deeply rural. Encompasses the fertile Vale of Aylesbury and a low sandy ridge to the valley of the River Ouse in the north.

Cambridgeshire – Encircled by a rim of low hills. Home to the University of Cambridge, founded in the 13th century. Another major landmark is the cathedral of Ely. The drainage of the Fens in the mid-17th century opened up new areas for grazing cattle and farming.

Huntingdonshire – Many medieval abbeys (now in ruins) were established within or adjacent to former marshlands, which were drained and cultivated by the 18th century. Mostly medieval stone bridges remain as testimony to the area's history.

Norfolk – A rich farming county in Eastern England. Known for Norwich Castle, not to mention Sandringham (the Norfolk home of the royal family). One of my relatives lives here!

Oxfordshire – Landlocked county. Includes parts of three Areas of Outstanding Natural Beauty. In the north-west lie the Cotswolds, to the south and south-east are the open chalk hills of the North Wessex Downs and wooded hills of the Chilterns.

Suffolk – Coastline has fine sandy beaches and crumbling cliffs (400 homes of a former town, Dunwich, washed into the sea in 1347 and again in 1570). The northwestern corner of Suffolk forms part of the reclaimed Fens marshland and is below sea level. East of the Fens is Breckland, an area with sand, heath, and long lines of trees.

11

TOWN OR COUNTRY?

At this point in your brainstorming, you need to drill down further. Do you want to set your story in a village like Elizabeth Bennett's modest home is, in *Pride & Prejudice?* Or a grand estate like *Emma's?* Would you like your characters to rusticate in a resort town such as Bath? Or descend upon London for the Season (capitalized to differentiate between the London Social Season and seasons of the year)?

You could set your story in a combination of settings, including travel, if the plot requires it. Otherwise, focus on one main setting, so you can add in secondary characters in a fleshed-out place. One positive off-shoot of interesting side personalities is that your plot will also expand and be enriched by the additions.

For example, in *Lady Serena's Choice*, I knew I wanted the story to take place along the coast, away from London. I read up on real estates in England to see how an estate would fit in with a nearby village and discovered in my research that oftentimes, a village revolves around the needs of an estate (like Downton Abbey).

Let's talk about each setting and their possibilities.

Village

A village historically sprung up around a manor, castle, or country estate. Servants and other hired hands lived in the village; the village supplied the retail needs of the manor and staff. Here are some landmarks to include in your fictional village: an inn, brewer, a local pub, church, vicarage, farms, village shops such as grocer, baker, haberdasher and shoemaker.

A pub is almost the equivalent of an inn. It's possible for there to be a pub and an inn in a village. Inns were places where people changed horses, where the stagecoach stopped, and where you could get accommodations. Pubs were merely drinking places.

Residents of a Village

Luckily for the modern author, British parishes faithfully recorded their histories. Here is an example of one such parish, based on information from the 1841 Census.

Appleby Magna is a village and civil parish in Leicestershire and Derbyshire, England.

Gentry. Comprising a handful of families, the gentry (Squire) occupied a prominent position in the Regency parish. They consisted of landowners who could live entirely off rental income and didn't work for a living. These families enjoyed wealth, hereditary title (lower titles of baronet, knight, esquire and gentleman addressed as Mr. and who didn't sit in the House of Lords), office and land-holding. Even their seating arrangements in the parish church reflected their status. (Think of the 2020 Emma film when Mrs. Elton took the first pew from Emma and her father.)

One such family, the Moores, bequeathed such luxury goods such as fine furniture, leaded glass, and painted wall hangings. They mostly derived their wealth from farming.

Clergy. Documents from the 1600s show a rector earning income from church lands including rent from two cottages. He also drew support of 25 acres of arable field strips and several small parcels of pasture, orchard and meadow. His dwellings included "five bays of kitchens and outbuildings," the equivalent of a prosperous husbandman or yeoman. (For more details on this gentle-manly profession, read the Chapter "The Gentleman Professions")

Yeoman. Generally refers to a farmer who owns his own piece of land as opposed to being a tenant farmer.

Husbandmen. Farmers who are less prosperous than the Yeoman.

Craftworkers. Blacksmiths, clothworkers, shoemak-ers, drapers, dressmakers, farriers, harness maker, wheel-wright, gamekeeper (looking after the squire's game), gardener.

Labourers. Sons of smallholders (those who owned or managed agricultural property smaller than a farm) worked as labourers while waiting to inherit the family holding (if the family owned it), or to make enough money to be husbandmen.

Country Estate

A large house in the English countryside, also referred to as the great house, stately home, mansion, castle, manor, court, or palace. It was the source of employment for hundreds of people near the estate. Due to intermarriage among the aristocracy, they often owned several of these country estates. Some would visit each according to season: grouse shooting in Scotland, pheasant shooting and fox hunting in England.

Minor county houses belonged to landed gentry. Similar to the larger estates, village life revolved around the house, but usually an owner only owned one.

Townhouse

The standard London townhouse of the 18th century was made of brick, with a flat façade. Each of its four or five floors had regularly-spaced sash windows. It was not a separate building, but rather a row of houses. Example of Regency townhouses included Mayfair and Bath. New Town in Edinburgh, Scotland, is not in England but gives a good view of what houses would have been like.

My editor recounts, "In my times in England, the most I ever saw was four levels. The basement or ground floor that had the kitchen and scullery, and sometimes rooms for the housekeeper and butler as well as rooms where the staff dined; the ground floor or second story that had the drawing room, dining room, parlor, etc.; the third story which usually had bedrooms; and the attic which housed the staff. Not saying there couldn't have been five, but that would have been unusual."

Often a canopy covered the front door, with front steps leading up to it, and the houses were built at pavement level without a front garden. For the working class, the ground floor sometimes served as a shop or business front.

12

THE ANNUAL REGENCY CALENDAR

WHICH MONTH or months would you like to set your story in?

For my first Regency romance, I needed to get the heroine stranded in a snowstorm so I made sure to set part of the story in the winter. The one thing I did *not* do was to play up the Christmas component in my book.

In hindsight, I should have done so, as Christmas romances are popular among readers. I might not have emphasized the holiday because, in contrast to the Victorian period, Christmas itself wasn't the big celebration in Regency England but rather the days leading up to Christmas, as well as Twelfth Night (January 6).

It's okay. Live and learn. That's the beauty of self-publishing. You can always do better the next time around. I might, in the future, do a bonus Christmas scene for my newsletter subscribers.

You can write a book practically every month around holidays. Here's a list to jumpstart some of your brainstorming.

January

1- New Year's Day

6- Twelfth Night – Also known as the Christian Epiphany, it is a Feast day celebrating the coming of the Magi. People exchange gifts, as well as host revels, masquerades and balls. Twelfth day cakes with colored sugar and spun figures were served. Got so rowdy, it was outlawed by Queen Victoria in the 1870s.

February

2- Candlemas – Named after the tradition of lighting candles to celebrate the presentation of the Christ Child in the temple.

14- Valentine's Day

March

Lent – The word is derived from an old English word meaning "lengthen." Lent is observed in spring, when the days begin to get longer.

Widely honored in the Regency, this Catholic tradition started on Ash Wednesday and ended on Easter. At Lent, people refrained from eating cakes, pastries, dairy, fats, as well as avoided meat on Friday. Maundy Thursday, commemorating the Last Supper, starts off the Easter celebrations. Parliament didn't start until after Easter or they took a break for Lent and Easter.

Easter - Falls on a different date every year, any time between March 22 and April 25. Though a Christian holiday, the day Easter falls on is determined by the Jewish calendar. This is because in the Bible, the death, burial, and resurrection of Jesus Christ happened after the Jewish festival of Passover, and followers wanted it to be celebrated as such.

March/April – Start of the Season in London.

25- Lady Day – Traditional day to hire farm laborers for upcoming planting and harvesting seasons. Also the Feast of the Annunciation (Angel Gabriel appears to the Virgin Mary).

April

23- St. George's Day, or Georgemas – In memory of St. George, England's patron saint. The anniversary of his death was considered England's national day. Legend has it he was a Roman soldier who slayed a dragon and saved a princess.

May

1- May Day – The halfway point between the spring equinox and the summer solstice. Day for dance and song, to celebrate the sprouting of sown fields. Traditionally, young couples paired today, though not yet for their wedding. That would come later, at Midsummer Day (June 24). Six weeks between May 1 and Midsummer gave the couple a chance to get to know each other.

June

24- Midsummer Day – Around the time of the summer solstice. This marked the halfway point between planting and harvest.

June / July

End of the London Season.

August

Lammas, or loaf mass – Halfway point between the summer solstice and autumn equinox. Celebration of harvesting grain (barley and oats), it marked the harvest of the first wheat or corn (grains such as wheat and barley) crop. Later transformed by the church into the feast of first fruits. "Loaf mas" (Old English half, "loaf," and maesse, "mass" or "feast") later turned "Lammas." After the loaf was blessed, the farmers divided it into four blocks and put each in barn corners to protect the newly harvested crop. Lammas bread was shaped into wheat, owl and corn dollies. Corn dollies were made from stalks of wheat, oats and rye, nothing like the American Indian corn doll.

September

29- Michaelmas – Around the time of the fall equinox. Harvest started on this day, with fairs and festivals.

October

31- Hallows' Eve – This is a Celtic tradition and was not celebrated in England except perhaps in Cornwall. If celebrated, All Hallows' Eve featured food, drink, and games that usually revolved around foretelling the future.

November

1-A Hallow's Day or All Saints Day - A Christian solemnity celebrated in honor of all the saints, known and unknown

2- Feast of All Souls or All Souls Day - Similar to The

Day of the Dead), this is a celebration of the faithful departed.

5- Guy Fawkes Day - At dusk, villagers start bonfires, set off fireworks, and burn an effigy of Guy Fawkes, celebrating his failure to blow up Parliament and James I.

11- Feast of St. Martin or Martinmas

30- Saint Andrew's Day (patron saint of Scotland, celebrated across Europe)*

In late fall and November, landed gentry dined on wild fowl and domestic poultry. Also beef, venison and pork. Winter vegetables: carrots, turnips, parsnips, potatoes, leeks, cabbage, celery and lettuces. Walnuts and chestnuts came into season.

December

Stir it up Sunday – Sunday before the beginning of Advent – The family makes Christmas puddings which needed to age (wrapped in brandy-moistened cloth to ripen). They were then served at Christmas dinner.

They also put little surprises in them such as silver coins (for wealth), tiny wishbones (for good luck), a silver thimble (for thrift), a ring (for marriage), or an anchor (for safe harbor) into the mixture, and when served, whoever got the lucky serving, could keep the charm.

Fourth Sunday before Christmas – Advent

6- St. Nicholas Day

21- St. Thomas Day – Elderly women (often widows) go 'a'thomasing' at more well-off neighbors for gifts of food or money

24- Christmas Eve

25- Christmas Day – Originated as a winter solstice festival. It celebrates rest and gathering fertility for sowing and reaping. This Celtic tradition later blended with the Christian celebration of the birth of Jesus.

26- St. Stephen's Day, or Boxing Day – Donated items were boxed up and given to tenants. Servants usually were given the day off. The well-off often held a sort of open house for less fortunate neighbors.

31- New Year's Eve

13

THE LONDON SEASON

The London season took place January to July. (Some authors end their Seasons in June.) Its commencement coincided with the start of Parliament (the dates of which changed every year), when upper class families moved back to London from their country seats. Some didn't come to town until March or April, usually after Easter. At that time, they took up lodgings in a rented or owned townhouse in the fashionable neighborhood of Mayfair, Knightsbridge or Belgravia.

Families with girls of marriageable age seized upon this opportunity to circulate in the myriads of balls, dances, assemblies, plays, and other entertainments, spotlighting their daughters for the marriage market. Those who were not part of the upper crust also had the chance to snag a wealthy husband or wife.

Parliament's end of session varied from year to year but was usually June or July. Most of the ladies returned to their country houses sometime in mid to late June because London was hot and smelly in the summer, so the social Season ended then. After parliament ended, the landowners had crops to oversee, meetings with their agents, and stewards, so they went to their country homes. During the summer, the nobility had house parties and once they took care of business at home, they sometimes went to the seashore or to Bath.

14

———

ALMACK'S

A VOUCHER to the exclusive Almack's, founded by William Almack, was sought after for the season. In 1765 Almack built a suite of assembly rooms in King's Street, St James's. For a ten-guinea subscription a series of weekly (Wednesday night) balls was given for twelve weeks. An elite group of six or seven wealthy and influential patronesses met every Monday night to determine who would be allowed into the hallowed halls.

The lady patronesses issued cards which were 2.5 inches by 3.5 inches, inscribed as follows: "Ladies Voucher Almack's, Deliver for (guest), Tickets for the Balls on the Wednesdays in (month) (year)." A patroness initialed the bottom right with a seal on the bottom left.

At Almack's death in 1781, his niece, Mrs. Willis, took over with "Willis's Rooms." As with Almack's, the establishment ceased in 1863.

The popularity of Almack's started to decline in 1825. Prince Puckler-Muskau, a German nobleman visiting London in April of that year, wrote: "The first Almack's ball took place this evening; and from all I had heard of this celebrated assembly, I was really curious to see it: but never were my expectations so disappointed. It was not much better than at Brighton. A large bare room, with a bad floor, and ropes round it, like the space in an Arab camp parted off for the horses; two or three naked rooms at the side, in which were served the most wretched refreshments; and a company into which, spite of the immense difficulty of getting tickets, a great many 'Nobodies' had wriggled; in which the dress was generally as tasteless as the tournure was bad; – this was all. In a word, a sort of inn-entertainment: – the music and the lighting the only good things. And yet Almack's is the culminating point of the English world of fashion."

At its height, Almack's boasted a great ballroom (90 feet long by 40 feet wide by 30 feet high) serenaded by an orchestra, with card rooms and supper rooms (typically 65 feet by 40 feet by 20 feet high).

15

———————

DANCING

Bowing is a traditional Regency practice. At a ball, participants bowed upon entering or leaving a room, at the beginning and end of every dance, and when greeting a person one wished to acknowledge. Females did not stand up for more than two consecutive dances with the same partner. Only those young ladies who were "out" danced and then only with an acceptable partner, which was usually someone she already knew, or to whom she had been formally introduced.

To avoid any suggestion of impropriety, dances were initially limited in music to English country dances and Scottish reels. This changed some time after the declaration of the Regency, when first the quadrille and then the waltz, were introduced. These were first danced at Almack's in 1813. By 1837, only the gallopade and the waltz were danced at the Almack's balls.

Waltz – Originally a rural dance that came to fashion in Vienna in the 1780s, the waltz reached England in 1791.

Watch the Hampshire Regency Dancers perform the dance on Youtube.

Considered risqué for quite a while after its introduction in the Regency, each dance number was basically choreographed. People learned the steps to the most popular dance numbers with dance masters before they came "out." Each song had a title, and a routine or choreography.

The word "waltz" refers to the music, usually in a 3/4 (three main beats per measure) time-signature; but the associated dancing figures were those of any other English Country Dance. The dance has been described this way: a gentleman takes a lady in a circle, with his right hand at her waist, her hand on his upper arm or shoulder, and his left hand holding her right hand.

Other "rules" of the dance included:

- Any number of couples may dance.
- Partners should embrace by the fingertips or by the elbows.
- Embracing by the waist is a less genteel (but common) waltz hold.
- The music changes speed throughout the dance, faster and slower.
- There is a risk of dizziness.

Country dance – Regency Dances describes the dance, performed in couples, made up of a man and woman, the male partners in one long line with the ladies in another facing them:

"A typical Country Dance formation involves the

leading couple dancing with the two couples below them, they're sometimes referred to as the first, second, and third couples; each couple will have a distinct role in each dance. The first couple will typically progress one position down the line during the figures, changing places with the second couple; the next iteration of the dance begins with them progressed one place, and dancing with a new second and third couple."

A number of Regency-era films depict country dances, but my favorite is from the 2005 *Pride & Prejudice*.

Scottish Reel – The Scottish reel is a variety of country dance performed in sets of two or more couples. The music is in quick 2/4 or 4/4 time. Watch the 19th Century Scotch Reels perform this dance.

Quadrille – Fashionable in London in the second half of the 1810s, the quadrille usually involved eight dancers in a square formation. It was named after a military term where four mounted horsemen performed such a formation. By the 1820s, the quadrille might be danced by twelve to sixteen dancers.

Paul Cooper of Regency Dances writes, "The couple at the head of a Quadrille is referred to as the 1st Couple, and they lead the dance. The Quadrille figures are repeated either twice or four times to allow each couple a chance to lead the dance in turn. The second couple to lead is the couple opposite the 1st Couple, and then the couple to the right of the 1st Couple, and finally the couple to the left of the 1st Couple. A simple counter-clockwise numbering system was also used during this same period (as used in typical Cotillion dances), so either sequence can be authentic."

Gallopade – The gallopade, or galop for short, is named after the fastest running gait of a horse. It is a lively country dance combining a *glissade* with a *chassé* on alternate feet, in a fast 2/4 time. Keeping one's feet is crucial. Watch it danced by Compagnie Révérences on Youtube.

16

REGENCY HOUSE PARTY

As my next book is set in the countryside, I read up with interest about the Regency House Party.

Thrown by wealthy families in their country estates, the House Party was a time-honored tradition. Held at the end of the Season and often coinciding with the hunt, a half-dozen to twenty guests converged upon a beautiful country house with its spacious grounds for anywhere from three to four guests, typically Thursday or Friday until Monday. Some sources say they went as long as twenty days. The length came about because travel was slow and difficult over poorly-maintained roads.

At a House Party, friends gathered; politics informally discussed; and matches between eligible ladies and gentlemen where engineered by crafty hostesses.

House Parties cost a pretty penny. Guests were feted with lavish meals and entertainment. A "simple" buffet breakfast included eggs, fruits, pastries, jam, cold cuts and toast. Luncheons could be held informally outdoors or formally as dinner. There was afternoon tea, after which guests changed for dinner, with everyone converging again at four o'clock.

The men would have been busy earlier in the day hunting or shooting. The ladies, on the other hand, would have been visiting, writing letters, or embroidering. If they walked outside, it was always with hats and gloves.

Guests (men and ladies alike) could indulge in games like croquet, lawn tennis, archery and shuttlecock. Indoors, they played word games, charades, and card games.

After dinner, the ladies retired to the drawing room. The men drank port and smoked cheroots. Afterward, everyone came together once again for cards, music, dancing or more games.

17

WEATHER & CLIMATE

Marc deSantis of Jane Austen Centre writes of fickle British weather in the late eighteenth century. "The winters were often very cold, and the springs very wet and late in arriving. Summers could be either very dry or cold and wet."

Most parts of England are cloudy and rainy most of the year, with some subtle variations. The following observations on British weather are from Climates to Travel. The rainfall amount is measured in inches for the year. Once you determine your exact location (if based on a real place), you can research weather further.

By Region

Different parts of the United Kingdom experience slightly different regional climates.

North West - Cool summers, mild winters, heavy rain all year.

North East - Cool summers, cold winters, steady rain all year

South East - Warm summers, mild winters, light rain all year, especially summer

South West - Warm summers, mild winters, heavy rain all year, especially winter

By Season
<u>Winter</u>

Cold and cloudy, sometimes foggy, sometimes windy. The eastside, including London, is more prone to snowfall. These snowy or freezing periods are typically short-lived. The mildest area is south-western England (Devon and Cornwall). Snowfalls and frosts are rare.

<u>Spring</u>

Very cool with a gradual temperature increase. Rainfall is still frequent but it's not as abundant as in autumn and winter. Spring is the sunniest period of the year. Clouds are a daily presence. It's not as windy.

In May, England is blanketed with flowers. June is pleasant. The days are long and gardens are blooming, thanks to avid British gardeners. Occasional rain and showers.

<u>Summer</u>

At 23°C (73°F), London gets warm. (Relatively speaking. In Utah where I live, temperatures can spike into the 100s.) Southern England can have hot periods, where Mediterranean currents from Spain can raise temperatures to 32°C (90°F). More rain falls in the north than the south.

Thunderstorms can come on especially inland and southern areas, accompanied by wind gusts. In Northern England, the sky is often cloudy.

The sea is cold even in the summer. In August, the Atlantic Ocean measures 17°C (63°F) in the English Channel and Cornwall.

<u>Autumn</u>

Gray and rainy, sometimes windy. First snow often comes in November.

British Weather in 1811-1820

Regency England had several climate-related events that would be worth noting as you choose your story timeline.

I've seen authors collaborate on a series based around The Last Great Frost Fair in 1814. Isn't that clever?

Pascal Bonenfant summarized the highlights of British weather from 1700 to 1849 on his website. Below, I zoned in on the years 1811-1820 but if your story takes place outside of those dates, I recommend you look up the years in Pascal's.

1811

January – The River Thames froze over.
    May – Thunderstorms for 9 days in the London area.
    September – Fog for 7 days in the south / London.

1812

March – Foot-deep snowfall around Edinburgh. Winds brought snowdrifts.
    Spring & Summer – Notably cold. The coldest spring since 1799 and would not be cold again until 1837. Rainfall was excessive. The wetter than usual weather slowed germination of crops; sowing may have been impossible on heavier soils. Harvest year was delayed, and when it did commence, the yield was low. Harvest began around September 20, and was not finished until the second week of November.

· · ·

1813/1814

The Last Great Frost Fair - One of the four or five coldest winters in England. The last time the River Thames froze over sufficiently to hold a frost fair. Other frost fair years were: 1683-84, 1716, 1739-40 and 1789. The greatest frost of the 19th century began on December 27, 1813, accompanied by thick fog.

The removal of the old London Bridge in 1831 increased the Thames' flow. Freezing of the river has not happened since.

Great amounts of snowfall also characterized this winter. In Dublin the snowfall trapped people in their houses. Canterbury was stranded for at least six days. The Thames was frozen solid from January 31 to February 5. The frost fair began February 1, lasting for four days between London Bridge and Blackfriars Bridge. The ice was so thick that an elephant was led across the river just below Blackfriars Bridge.

For more details on the Frost Fair, here is a fun little write-up by Thames Leisure on it.

1815/1816

A severe winter

1816 & 1817

. . .

Two wet years with wet summers

1816

Summer – was called The Year without a Summer. A violent volcanic eruption of Tambora (Sumbawa Island / modern-day Indonesia) in April 1815 the East Indies threw dust and sulphur dioxide into the stratosphere, which affected the following summer. Grain harvests were late and continuous rain led to total failure of crops.

September & October - Sharp frost, snowdrifts. In NE Scotland, there was a great hurricane and snowstorm. Corn crops buried under the snow were so frozen they couldn't be thawed for the cattle.

1817

Summer - A wet summer across England and Wales. Another bad year across Scotland, with damaging frosts delaying harvest.

September – Fog for 7 days.

1818

January – Severe westerly gale damaged buildings in Edinburgh.

March- Very severe gales on March 4, 7, and 8. Notably wet across England and Wales.

Summer – Claimed to be the longest, driest and warmest in living memory. Followed by a wet autumn.

1819

May 30 – Severe frost affected large areas of Britain. Considerable plant damage reported as far apart as the Forest of Dean (Gloucestershire), Rugby and several places in Scotland.

October 22 – Snow across southern England including the London area. More snowfall in Surrey.

1820

January – Minus 23°C (-10°F) measured at Tunbridge Wells.

March 3-A report on a fire in Chatham mentions strong north-westwardly wind. A hurricane blew in from the River Medway.

18

LADIES' FASHION

REGENCY GOWNS WERE KNOWN for their high-waisted, natural figure. Ladies wore gloves outside the house. Inside, such as when making a social call, or on formal occasions such as a ball, the ladies removed them. Reticules, or small drawstring handbags, held personal items as ball gowns had no pockets. (Dresses had slits in the sides or pockets tied around the waist.) On their feet, they wore thin, flat fabric (silk or velvet), or leather slippers (in contrast to the high heeled shoes of much of the 1700s). Ladies also wore riding and walking boots.

Underneath the fashions, the ladies wore several layers of undergarments:

- Chemise or shift, a thin garment with tight, short sleeves and a low neckline, made of white cotton
- A pair of stays, though high-waisted classical fashions required no corset for the slight of figure. It was a much more comfortable version of the corset.

- Drawers, underpants with legs just below the knee, were worn by a few, and not until 1806. (And even then, the average lady did not wear these at all because they were considered masculine and therefore vulgar to wear.) Tied separately around the waist. Some ladies wore pantaloons under their riding habits.
- Sleeveless petticoat with a scooped neckline, fitted in the back with hooks and eyelets, buttons or tapes. Worn between the underwear and the outer dress.
- Stockings—often of a white or pale flesh color made of silk or knitted cotton, held up by garters below the knee.

How female Regency fashion evolved over the years

(Check out Pinterest for visual examples.)

<u>1790s</u>

Age of Undress, or casual and informal—a triumph over the brocades, lace and periwigs of the earlier 18th century. No one wanted to appear to be a member of the French aristocracy.

Dressing like Greek or Roman statues coming to life, following classical (e.g. Greek and Roman) ideals

Fillet-Greek classical hairstyle (fillet is a wire-stiffened string or braid of fabrics and/or pearls, twisted into an evening hairstyle)

Simple muslin chemise with ribbon, keeping arms bare

Sheer, empire silhouette with layered skirts in pastel fabrics (pinks, periwinkle blue, or lilacs). A mature matron could wear bolder colors such as purple, black, crimson, deep blue or yellow. Purple was rare and only used by the very rich. Real purple came from a shellfish. Green wasn't used much except in Victorian times and since the dye was made from arsenic, it was poisonous.

White or pastel was the most fashionable for ladies of all ages because it was a sign of status. It took work to keep them pristine. They clearly didn't work at manual labor or they'd stain their clothing.

Natural makeup. Very few who weren't on the stage wore make-up, and those who did were usually older and considered eccentric.

Accessories: hats, turbans, gloves, jewelry, small handbags (reticules), shawls, handkerchiefs, parasols, fans

1800s

Short hair, or, if long, masses of curls sometimes pulled back into a chignon

White hats, trim, feathers, and lace

Egyptian and Eastern influenced jewelry and apparel

Shawls in cashmere, silk or muslin for the summer, popular in Paisley patterns

Hooded overcoats

1810s

. . .

Soft, subtle, sheer classical drapes

Raised back waist of high-waisted dresses

Short (high-waisted) single-breast jackets called spencers

Morning dress, worn at home in the afternoons as well as mornings, or while making calls, high-necked and long-sleeved

Walking dress

Evening dress – Both sexes changed for the evening meal and entertainments. Women's gowns, mostly made of muslin for daywear and sometimes of silk for evening dress, were cut low and sported short sleeves, baring bosoms. Bared arms were covered by long white gloves.

Riding habits

Hair parted in the center, with tight ringlets over the ears and across the forehead like curly bangs

1820s

Lower waistlines, elaborate hem and neckline decoration

Cone-shaped skirts

Pinched sleeves

19

MEN'S FASHION

MEN STYLED their hair with hair wax, and grew mutton chops as a style of facial hair. Around their necks, men wore a cravat—a large, usually starched square or triangle of linen or silk folded into a band.

On their feet for daywear, they wore Hessian boots with heart-shaped tops and tassels. After the Duke of Wellington defeated Napoleon at Waterloo in 1815, Wellington boots —with knee-high tops in front and cut lower in back— became popular. For riding, gentlemen wore the jockey boot with a turned-down cuff of lighter colored leather. Court shoes—slippers or pumps—for evening and especially for dancing, entered the fashion scene as trousers were introduced.

For undergarments, men wore shirts that reached to their knees. Some men of the ton, including the Prince of Regent, wore tightly laced stays. Later in the period, they wore drawers, a garment like shorts with a drawstring and buttoned flaps.

How male Regency fashion evolved over the years

1790s

Riding dress: snug leather breeches with a tie and buttons at the knee and fall front
Breeches for casual wear or pantaloons for formal wear
Stockings and buckled shoes
Double-breasted waistcoat in white or color with embroidery
White, linen shirts (sometimes with ruffles and lace on neck or sleeves)
Tall, slightly conical hat Tailcoats of all colors with gold buttons
Cloaks
The Dandy, a man who tries to look effortlessly put-together. More refined and sober than the fop. Less refined than the Macaroni.
Dark colors (but cut from rich, vivid fabrics)
Start of the cutaway coat sytle

1800s

Linen shirts with high collars
Tall hats over short and wigless hair, á la Titus or Bedford Crop
Older men, military officers, lawyers, judges, physicians,

and servants still wore wigs and powder. Powdered hair was still required in court.

Elaborate embroidery in formal court suits

Coats cutaway in the front with long tails

1810s

Plain white or horizontally striped waistcoats

1820s

Trousers were just coming into fashion during the late Regency but didn't catch on until this decade

Tailcoats gave way to frock coats, which tapered to the back rather than being cut straight at the waist and falling like our modern tuxedo

Overcoats or greatcoats with contrasting collars of fur or velvet

Wellington boots; jockey boots

20

THE GENTLEMAN PROFESSIONS

Primogeniture. Say that fast, I dare you.

It is Latin for "first born." (Honestly, why didn't someone just say that?)

That basically was the practice among the gentry of giving the oldest son the entire estate of his parents (or nearest ancestor).

If no direct male heir exists, then it goes up the line to a grandfather and back down to the closest male heir. If there isn't one in that generation, then it goes up to the great-grandfather and back down until one is found, and so forth. If there really are no male living heirs, then the land goes to the king and the title, if one exists, goes extinct. Daughters get no part of the entailed estate (a settlement of the inheritance of property over a number of generations so that it remains within a family or other group). They can be left money in wills, but they were expected to marry and their husband provide. Any money of theirs goes to the husband. Primogeniture created a dilemma for the younger sons. It didn't change the fact they were gentlemen of noble birth who needed to earn a living (money doesn't grow on trees, even on the ducal estate) but not in manual labor. That doesn't leave a younger son with a lot of choices, does it? Luckily, they had the following options:

Officers

Readers of Regency often will come across references to the Napoleonic War. The Napoleonic era began on November 9, 1799 when French Emperor Napoleon Bonaparte seized control of the French revolutionary government. Britain and its allies went to war against France until July 1815, when the British defeated Napoleon—and France—at Waterloo. Against this backdrop, a soldier returning from the Napoleonic Wars makes for a dashing Regency hero.

Men from wealthy families could purchase a military officer commission in the Army, which was returned to them (like a nest egg) upon retirement. As they only accepted a tiny honoraria, their parents often gave them an allowance. But not all the officers were from the upper class. Some were from other lower classes, commonly promoted by merit rather than a bought commission.

Clergy

In a wealthy family, typically the first son inherited the land and the title, the second went into the military, and the third or fourth into church or law.

As I grew up Catholic, the thought of clergy being the desirable hero in a romantic novel still fills me with guilt.

But since most of the clergy in Regency England belonged to religions (like the predominant Anglican Church as well as the Methodist Church) where they could marry, we are good!

Really, if you think about it, clergy would make for some of the most appealing beta-type heroes. Strong convictions but scripture-based, serious but with an often secret fun-loving side. A calming personality unless they are pounding the pulpit for emphasis.

So what did it take for a gentleman to be ordained in the Anglican church? He would go to a prestigious university like Oxford or Cambridge to get his degree (not necessarily in theology like in modern times). Which made it difficult if not next to impossible for a poor man to be clergy, unless they get a patron, or someone wealthy who can sponsor their education.

A clergyman began his career at age 23, as a deacon, assisting an ordained clergyman. At 24, he could be fully ordained and eligible to be in charge of a parish.

Yup, I know. Ideal romance novel hero age.

After ordination, a priest (curate, vicar or rector) would be called Mr. (Surname). A vicar presided over a living (a parish church). For payment, the parish would give him ten per cent (could be as little as £50 a year) of the parish's produce and livestock. Whoever owned the living in the area (think Lady Catherine in *Pride & Prejudice*) also supplied the vicar the living. During the Regency era, a vicar position was a lifetime post, unless he wanted to retire.

His duties included holding church service (as long as three hours) on Sundays (where he delivered a sermon) and hold Holy Communion (on special feast days, but not every Sunday). The clergyman officiated over baptisms, marriages and funerals, as well as visited the sick. He also coordinated other charity and parish maintenance at parish meetings.

If you want to read a good vicar romance, check out Sarah M. Eden's *The Heart of a Vicar*.

The Law

Solicitor and barrister are generally accepted as meaning Regency lawyers.

Men who pursued this profession could work as a barrister or solicitor. A barrister represented clients in court and was considered a gentleman. They were not salaried, but rather received a gratuity.

A solicitor prepared contracts and other legal duties and was considered a member of the middle class. They acted as broker between clients who needed a trial lawyer and the barrister, taking a cut of the gratuity as their fee.

For further reading, Rory Muir lays out an excellent explanation of barristers vs. attorneys / solicitors in *Gentlemen of Uncertain Fortune*.

The Doctor

As with the Law, there were two types of doctor: the physician, who was considered a gentleman, and a surgeon, who were considered middle class. Why the distinction? The physician had more education and did not apprentice. The surgeon worked alongside a more experienced surgeon as an apprentice. The physician would be called "Doctor" whereas the surgeon would be called "Mister."

The true distinction came due to their birth. Were they born gentlemen? Another distinction was that the doctor would avoid touching people (which made him higher class) but the surgeon would. The physician treated his patients by asking detailed questions and prescribing treatment.

In the country, one usually called for an apothecary.

Many of the physician degrees came from the University of Edinburgh and Glasgow as well as London. Also, many surgeons and physicians were part of the Navy.

A good physician romance is Sally Britton's *The Gentleman Physician*.

~

Author's note: for my first Regency romance novella, I chose to make the hero a stable boy. Go figure. But I am set for having a gentleman hero the next time around!

21

SOCIAL CLASSES

THE HIERARCHY in Regency society was structured, from top to bottom:

Monarch – The Prince Regent George, Prince of Wales

Royalty – his wife Caroline, Princess of Wales, daughter Princess Charlotte, and their close relatives

Nobility – rank, from highest to lowest: duke (duchess), marquess (marchioness), earl (countess), viscount (viscountess), baron (baroness).

Gentry – owns at least 300 acres of land. This class includes baronets, knights, country landowners (often extremely wealthy) and gentlemen of property and good birth without title (males were referred to as Esquire).

. . .

Middle Classes – financiers, merchants (referred to as cits, a derogatory term for the noveau riche) , industrialists, as well as wealthy physicians, lawyers, engineers, higher clergy and farmers. Also included shopkeepers, teachers, builders, the lesser clergy, civil servants, clerks, and innkeepers.

Artisans and Tradespeople – skilled workers and craftsmen

Servants –
Upper servants consisted of, for the men: steward, groom of the chambers, butler, and valet. For the women: housekeeper, head housemaid, and lady's maid.
Lower servants, for the men: footman, coachman, groom, stable boy. For the women: housemaid, kitchen maid, scullery maid, and laundry maid.

Laboring Poor – laborers, peddlers, chimney sweeps, ordinary soldiers and sailors

Paupers – include those who, due to old age or sickness, could not obtain work.

To climb the social ladder, one could marry, accumulate great wealth, land an estate, or acquire a title. After a couple

generations, a descendant of a commoner is usually accepted into the upper class.

22

UNDERSTANDING TITLES

Here are a few of the most common titles used in Regency and examples. Be sure to triple-check your title usage as readers aren't too forgiving if an author messes this up. But, and a big but, do not let this overwhelm you, as it did me, looking at the charts when starting out in the genre. Pick a title and look up its different iterations. You do not need to master all the titles from the get-go. I imagine it would take several books to understand this. It is a wonder they all got this straight in the Regency Era (and even into modern times)!

Of note, a person's given name could be used only by close friends and family. A person of higher rank could use the given name of a lower class acquaintance, but not the other way around. The eldest daughter in a family would be addressed "Miss" + last name. Her sisters would be "Miss" + given name.

For this chapter, I used Susanne Dietze's method on *Lady Serena's Choice* main and spin-off characters. For a more extensive guide to forms of address, check out her blog post (http://www.susannedietze.com/british-forms-of-address.html) . My editor swears by Laura Chinet's summary charts.

DUKE

Duke (Frederick Clarke, the Duke of Delaval)
    Introduced as: His Grace the Duke of Delaval
    Referred to as: His Grace (by inferiors), Duke (by peers)

Duchess (Catherine Clarke, the Duchess of Delaval)
    Introduced as: Her Grace the Duchess of Delaval
    Referred to as: Her Grace
    In Speech: Your Grace (by inferiors), Duchess (by peers)
    Dowager: Her Grace Margaret*, Duchess of Delaval or Her Grace the Dowager Duchess of Delaval
    *Catherine and Margaret are different individuals.

NOTE: The term dowager for any lady was only used if people needed to differentiate between her and her daughter-in-law, or in written correspondence. Otherwise, they'd drop "Dowager" in speech.

Eldest Son (Quinn Clarke, The Marquess of Leitham -- courtesy title)
    Introduced as: The Marquess of Leitham
    In Speech: Lord Leitham, my lord

· · ·

Younger Son (Ransom Clarke)
    Introduced as: Lord Ransom Clarke
    In Speech: Lord Ransom

Daughter (Serena Clarke)
    Introduced as: Lady Serena Clarke
    In Speech: Lady Serena

MARQUESS (pronounced MAA-kwis)

Marquess (Devin Moore, the Marquess of Fenwick)
    Introduced as: The Marquess of Fenwick
    Referred to as: Lord Fenwick
    In Speech: Lord Fenwick, my lord
    Referred to by employee as: my lord (to his face) or your lordship (in reference to)

Marchioness (Amelie Moore, the Marchioness of Fenwick)
    Introduced as: The Marchioness of Fenwick
    Referred to as: Lady Fenwick
    In Speech: Lady Fenwick, my lady
    Referred to by employee as: my lady (to her face), her ladyship (in reference to)
    Dowager: Teresa, Marchioness of Fenwick, or the Dowager Marchioness of Fenwick

Eldest Son (Bramwell Moore, the Earl of Wessom -- courtesy title)

Introduced as: The Earl of Wessom
In Speech: Lord Wessom

Younger Son (Edward Moore)
Introduced as: Lord Edward Moore
In Speech: Lord Edward

Daughter (Daphne Moore)
Introduced as: Lady Daphne Moore
In Speech: Daphne Moore

EARL

Earl (Marcus Westwood, the Earl of Montrose)
Introduced as: The Earl of Montrose
Referred to as: Lord Montrose
In Speech: Lord Montrose, my lord
Referred to by employee as: my lord (to his face), his lordship (in reference to)
Signs letters: Montrose

Countess (Gabrielle Westwood, the Countess of Montrose)
Introduced as: The Countess of Montrose
Referred to as: Lady Montrose
In Speech: Lady Montrose, my lady
Referred to by employee as: my lady, or her ladyship (in reference to)

Dowager: Maria, Countess of Montrose or The Dowager Countess of Montrose

Eldest Son (Leo Westwood, the Viscount Harford--courtesy title)
    Introduced as: The Viscount Harford
    In Speech: Lord Harford

Younger Son (The Honorable Bertram Westwood)
    Introduced as: Mr. Bertram Westwood
    In Speech: Mr. Westwood

Daughter (Diana Westwood)
    Introduced as: Lady Diana Westwood
    In Speech: Lady Diana

VISCOUNT (pronounced VAI-count)

Viscount (Jasper Lennox, the Viscount Ridgewater)
    Introduced as: The Viscount Ridgewater
    Referred to as: Lord Ridgewater
    In Speech: Lord Ridgewater, my lord
    Referred to by employee as: my lord, or his lordship (in reference to)

Viscountess (Cecilia Lennox, the Viscountess Ridgewater)
    Introduced as: The Viscountess Ridgewater

Referred to as: Lady Ridgewater

In Speech: Lady Ridgewater, my lady

Referred to by employee as: my lady, or her ladyship (in reference to)

Dowager: Patrice, Viscountess Ridgewater, or The Dowager Viscountess Ridgewater

Eldest Son (The Honorable Bridger Lennox)
    Introduced as: Mr. Bridger Lennox
    In Speech: Mr. Lennox

Younger Son (The Honorable Nathaniel Lennox)
    Introduced as: Mr. Nathaniel Lennox
    In Speech: Mr. Lennox

Eldest Daughter (The Honorable Honor Lennox)
    Introduced as: Miss Honor Lennox
    In Speech: Miss Lennox

Younger Daughter (The Honorable Faith Lennox)
    Introduced as: Miss Faith Lennox
    In Speech: Miss Lennox

BARON

Baron (Victor Conway, Baron Lipcott)
    Introduced as: The Lord Lipcott

Referred to as: Lord Lipcott
In Speech: Lord Lipcott

Baroness (Chloe Conway, Baroness Lipcott)
    Introduced as: The Lady Lipcott
    Referred to as: Lady Lipcott, my lady
    In Speech: Lady Lipcott
    In Speech: Lady Lipcott
    Dowager: The Right Hon. the Dowager Lady Lipcott or
Caroline, Lady Lipcott

Son (The Honorable Samuel Conway)
    Introduced as: Mr. Samuel Conway
    In Speech: Mr. Samuel Conway

Eldest Daughter (The Honorable Sabrina Conway)
    Introduced as: Miss Sabrina Conway
    In Speech: Miss Conway

Younger Daughter (The Honorable Josephine Conway)
    Introduced as: Miss Josephine Conway
    In Speech: Miss Conway

23

DAILY LIFE

AFTER BREAKFAST WITH THE CHILDREN, the first job of the lady of the house would be to talk to the housekeeper. It would be important for them to communicate about the other servants, making sure they were doing their jobs properly and behaving correctly above and below stairs.

They would also discuss the evening meal. If visitors were expected, the lady would choose meals that were lavish and unusual. After these matters were dealt with the wife would then check through the household accounts. Bills for meat, candles, and flour would usually be paid weekly. When the early morning activities were finished, the social whirl would begin! High society ladies would either receive calls or visit others. Morning calls were made at three or four in the afternoon. Tea was served at 5:00 p.m.

Note: this is not cut and dry, as some households—as in modern times—could have different schedules depending on household, status, habits, and personalities.

24

——————

SERVANTS

A SMALL BUT well-to-do household would employ between eight and twelve servants. Larger households, like a ducal estate, could have as many as fifty. Some would live in attic bedrooms and some above the stables. If these were full, they would sleep in the servants' hall and kitchen down on the ground floor (even though it was below street level; this was the modern equivalent of a basement).

The senior management included the steward, butler, housekeeper, and cook or chef. Here are their positions and responsibilities.

Steward – In a large estate, like a duke's household, managed the household staff.

Butler – Front door, messages and calling cards. Wine deliveries and rebottling. Glasses and silver plate, stored in his room, or "butler's pantry." Laid the table and supervised food service, took evening tea into the drawing room and locked the front door at night.

Housekeeper – Responsible for the female servants. Respectfully called Mrs., regardless of her marital status. Take orders from the lady of the house. Organize the daily food shopping for perishables. Supervise general tasks like mending and laundry. She also carried the keys to the house and to the safe where the china and silver were kept.

Cook – Cook for the family. Highest paid employee even above the steward and regarded separate from the domestic staff.

Lady's Maids – Serve the lady or ladies of the house directly. Help them dress and maintain their wardrobe.

Valets – Serve the gentleman of the house as barber. Help them dress and maintain their wardrobe.

Footmen – Clean boots and shoes, act as valet to the master (only if the valet was sick), look after the oil lamps and candles, polish the furniture in main rooms, and attend to the master or mistress when they were out in the carriage. They went on shopping expeditions to carry parcels. Served food and drinks during a party.

Chamber Maids / House Maids – Rise earliest to clean the grates and light the fires using a tinder box. Carry coal, and heat and carry water upstairs to bedrooms. Clean chamber pots, change bed linens and scrub floors.

Kitchen Maids – Light stoves and prepare meals.

Scullery Maids – Clean up in kitchen and after meals.

Outdoor Staff – Includes coachmen, grooms, gardener, and gamekeeper.

25

A DINNER MENU

Louis Simond, an American in Regency England, described a meal with his host and hostess thus: "The master and mistress of the house sit at each end of the table–narrower and longer than the French tables–the mistress at the upper end–and the places near her are the places of honour. There are commonly two courses and a dessert. I shall venture to give a sketch of a moderate dinner for ten or twelve persons. Although contemporary readers may laugh, I flatter myself it may prove interesting in future ages."

Here was the menu:

First course (not in order)

Oyster Sauce, Fish, Fowls, Soup, Vegetables, Roasted or Boiled Beef, Spinage (spinach?), Bacon, Vegetables

Second Course (not in order)

Creams, Ragout á la Francoise, Pastry, Cream, Cauliflowers, Game, Celery, Macaroni, Pastry.

. . .

Dessert (not in order)

Walnuts, Raisins and Almonds, Apples, Cakes, Pears, Oranges

"Soon after dinner the ladies retire, the mistress of the house rising first, while the men remain standing. Left alone, they resume their seats, evidently more at ease, and the conversation takes a different turn–less reserved–and either graver, or more licentious."

Dinner Etiquette

- A servant may be ignored at mealtimes.
- It was essential to dress for dinner.
- When going into dinner, the man of the house always escorted the highest-ranking lady present. The remaining dinner guests also paired up and entered the dining room in order of rank.
- Dinner guests were seated according to rank, with the highest-ranking lady sitting on the right-hand side of the male host, who always sat at the head of the table.
- When dining informally it was acceptable to talk across or round the table.
- At a formal dinner one did not talk across the dinner table but confined conversation to those

on one's left and right.
- Ladies were expected to retire to the withdrawing room after dinner, leaving the men to their port and their "male" talk.
- A hostess should never give the signal to rise from the table until everyone at the table had finished.
- It was acceptable to offer one's snuff-box to the company but not to ask for a pinch of snuff from anyone else.

26

CHILDREN

Children in Regency England fared differently depending on the social class they belonged to.

Working class children took employment in factories and textile mills at an early age. They did not go to school as education then was not free. Work around these large machines was dangerous and required them to put in 13 hour-days, six days a week. Labor conditions improved when laws passed in the early 19th century limited their work hours and assured more safety.

In contrast, upper class children were supervised by a nurse (the younger children), governess (older girls), and tutor (boys). Boys went on to a public school, meaning a school with other children such as Eaton or Harrow which they could enter as young as six, but not usually until they were ten or twelve.

First thing in the day, they dressed—boys and girls in dresses alike until they were a little older. Older boys wore breeches, while girls wore pantaloons under their dresses. As a gesture of respect for their elders, girls curtsied, while boys doffed their caps or hats.

. . .

Here is a typical day in an upper class Regency child's life:

Rise and dress for the day.

Eat breakfast with Mother.

Younger children played with the nurse. Governess taught the older girls. Tutor taught the older boys.

Tea with biscuits, crumpets, fruits, etc.

Nap for the younger children.

Day lessons, play and exercise.

Go out to the garden in the Square.

Eat a meal earlier than parents.

Bedtime.

27

NOTABLE LANDMARKS

Outside London

BATH, Somerset – In 1775, the original Roman baths in this Somerset town were discovered and restored. This created a big social whirl with lots of parties and balls. They also had assembly rooms for balls. Visitors, including Jane Austen from 1801 to 1806, flocked to the Pump Room to "take the waters."

Brighton – A town along the Sussex coast, Brighton became a popular resort destination.

In London

Covent Garden- Not a place where young women would go, even with escorts. In the mid-17th century, it started out as a small, open-air fruit-and-vegetable market on the south side of the fashionable square. By the 18th century, it became notorious for its abundance of brothels.

Hyde Park- Open every day of the year, from six in the

morning until nine at night. The park was just for walking, except for Rotten Row.

Rotten Row – A fashionable place to be seen riding your horse in Hyde Park. Anyone could ride a horse on Rotten Row, a broad track running some 4,541 feet along the south side of Hyde Park. The name is believed to be a corruption of La Route du Roi. Carriages, but not hackney nor stagecoaches, were also allowed there.

Mayfair – A highly desirable neighborhood. It was marked by Picadilly on the south, Oxford on the north, Park Lane on the west, and Regent Street on the east. Berkeley Square, Grosvenor Square and Hanover Square were landmarks within Mayfair.

Tattersall's – Founded in 1766 by Richard Tattersall who had been stud groom to a duke. A meeting place for sporting and betting men, as well as lively horse auctions.

Vauxhall Gardens – A public park in Kennington, London, on the south bank of the River Thames. From 1785 to 1859, it was a pleasure garden where the public could go and enjoy various attractions such as concerts, and fireworks. Drawing enormous crowds, couple took advantage of the shadowy paths for romantic assignations. It was quite daring for an upper-class woman to go there. It closed in 1840, re-opened in 1841, changed owners in 1842, and permanently closed in 1859.

White's Club – The oldest gentleman's club (private social club) in England, established in 1693. White's, as well as two other gentleman's clubs named Brooks's (yes, the extra s is supposed to be there) and Boodle's, provided aristocrats with a venue for gambling, which was illegal outside of members-only establishments.

From 1783 it was the unofficial headquarters of the Tory party, while the Whigs' club Brooks's was just down the road. A few managed to belong to both. The building featured a bow window on the ground floor. In the later 18th century, the table directly in front of it was taken up by fashion and social arbiter Beau Brummell, until he fled England to escape mounting debts in 1816.

28

HORSES, CARRIAGES AND TRAVEL

RIDING ON HORSEBACK IS, confessedly, one of the most graceful, agreeable, and salutary of feminine recreations. No attitude, perhaps, can be regarded as more elegant than that of a lady in the modern side-saddle; nor can any exercise be deemed capable of affording more rational and innocent delight, than that of the female equestrian. – A Young Lady's Equestrian Manual, published 1838

As an owner of horses for over a decade, I thought writing about horses in the Regency would be a breeze. Although I did know about horses, their care, and riding, I realized I still had a lot to learn.

Ladies rode side-saddle in a stylish riding habit. They started out riding astride on a pony or donkey (I can only imagine the comedy of the latter). Female adults seldom rode astride even in the country as it would be deemed scandalous. (I did have my heroine break convention because I could not picture her galloping over her family's estate or riding a foxhunt side saddle. Lady riders back then managed to ride side-saddle splendidly, perhaps even more securely because of the hooks for their legs.)

A large estate had a head groom who taught the daughters of the house how to ride. Several grooms were also in attendance to help with mounting or accompanying the misses out on the grounds.

About the time of the Regency period, the ideal English racing horse emerged—the Darley Arabian, Godolphin Barb and Byerley Turk were cross-bred to produce the Thoroughbred.

Apart from breeding them for races, foxhunting on these Thoroughbreds was a popular sport among the wealthy, often hosting their own events over their acres of property. They used English Hounds, which I discovered do not bay mournfully like their American counterparts, but rather emit shorter high-pitched barks.

Horse-Drawn Vehicles

Barouche – a four-wheeled carriage with two facing seats. The forward facing seat has a collapsible hood. Pulled by two or four horses, it had a driver's box seat in front.

Curricle – A fashionable open-air sporting vehicle with two wheels designed to be pulled by two horses and seating for no more than two. A groom or "tiger" could sit in a small seat in the rear.

· · ·

Phaeton – An open-air sporting vehicle with four wheels and seating for two.

Post chaise – Also known as traveling chariot. It was a small carriage pulled by two to four horses. Owned or hired by those who wish to travel privately. There is also a closed coach which is completely enclosed so it's better for long distances.

Gretna Green

Gretna Green, a city just past the English border into Scotland, was a famous wedding destination for eloping couples following the 1754 Marriage Act, which prevented couples under the age of 21 from marrying in England or Wales without their parents' consent. Since it was legal in Scotland to marry, couples began crossing the border into Scotland.

It bears mentioning at this point in the book because traveling there required quite substantial horsepower and multiple days. As a frame of reference, the distance between London to Gretna Green was roughly 350 miles. According to Jane Austen's World, it would have taken an eloping couple four days with frequent stops to change tired horses, rest for food, plus an overnight stop at an inn. Sometimes they just changed horses and drivers, traveling day and night—especially if an angry father was in hot pursuit. It was scandalous to elope. By the time they arrived, the girl was considered ruined.

29

THOUGHTS FROM A BRIT

Karen Pierotti is a British expatriate now living in Utah, USA, who writes under the pen name Karen M. Edwards.

by Karen Pierotti

I'VE ALWAYS ENJOYED READING Regency romances starting with Jane Austen and Georgette Heyer. But lately, I've also been lucky enough to read Regency romances from local authors and have been privileged to read some of their manuscripts. When reading those manuscripts there were a few subtle things I noticed as a Brit that Americans were not always aware of. I was happy to include my thoughts on the differences between the UK and the USA for Jewel's book.

The Country

Though Jewel is concentrating on Regency England, I'd like

to point out that there are three other countries (yes, countries, not counties): Northern Ireland (Eire or Ireland is its own country and not part of the UK, but it is part of the geographic British Isles), Scotland and Wales. Don't assume that things will be the same in say, Scotland as in England, especially with marriage. See my blog post (http://historicalhussies.blogspot.com/2019/05/tying-knot-in-regency-scotland.html)at Historical Hussies.

I'd also like to mention that counties would be the equivalent of states in the USA and are not similar to counties within states. Please note that not all counties use the -shire suffix which were Anglo-Saxon divisions from the 10th century.

The Terrain

If you have a bird's eye view or Google Earth (use this but imagine it with fewer built up places) view of the UK, you'd see different kinds of terrain, but in many areas it looks like a patchwork of small fields surrounded by hedges, with narrow winding roads running through it to the various hamlets, villages, towns, and cities. (Also bridges over rivers which had carriage traffic would be made of stone, not wood, though Thomas Telford was building bridges of iron during the Georgian/Regency period.)

Americans use the term "city" for most dwelling places. In the UK, technically a city was a place that had a cathedral; nowadays it depends on the size of the place. In Regency times your characters would encounter more towns and villages. Even London was called a town, so when people would say "I'm going to Town," it usually meant London. And just to confuse things, there's an area in London called the City which is now the banking area but was originally founded by the Romans and enlarged in Medieval times; it also had walls and gates though the walls were demolished in the mid-1700s. And there was the separate City of Westminster, but only known as Westminster, where Royalty lived and now the area of government. This area also includes upscale areas like Mayfair, Belgravia where nobility and gentry resided when Parliament was in session. This is an area your upper class characters would know well. There were a lot of houses being built in this area during Georgian and Regency times. Check out old maps of London from Vision of Britain which is also a good place to read up information on various towns and villages.

The US has many different types of terrain and it would depend on where one comes from how you would envision a forest. In the UK, the term forest and wood are differentiated while it seems to be used more interchangeably in the US. Read up on the distinction according to Woodland Trust (https://www.woodlandtrust.org.uk)

The modern day understanding of the term 'forest' refers to an area of wooded land, but this has not always been the case. The original medieval meaning was similar to a 'preserve', for example land that is legally kept for specific purposes such as royal hunting. So 'forests' were areas large enough to support species such as wolves and deer for game hunting and they encompassed other habitats such as heaths, open grassland and farmland.

The term woodland is also considered to be land covered with trees and vegetation, but in the UK woods tend to not be as large as forests. For example, Loch Arkaig pine forest in the Highlands of Scotland is 2,500 acres, while St. John's Woods in Devon is just three acres.

To be on the safe side, use the term "woods" which in England would mostly be deciduous with maybe a few pines. No deep dark forests with tall pine trees, and no maples and hickory, if you were ever to delve into such details. A landowner or a large estate would also plant and maintain woods as well as areas for hunting birds. So the landscape of a large estate might have woods (with possible glades/clearings in them), copses, a stand of trees, a grove, orchards, shrubbery, hedges, and perhaps an orangery (a green house where orange and other tender trees and plants). Check out the hunting laws of the time so that one of your characters could offer to let a visitor shoot on their estate as *Pride and Prejudice* and *Persuasion*.

Made-up Names for Towns/Villages

If you decide to make up a village or town, I would suggest picking a particular area (it would also make a difference how far away it was from London or Bath) and then playing around with variations. The names of places go back a long way. For example, a lot of the northeast of England was part of the Danelaw where the Danes ruled for about 100 years, and there are still places with names that end in -by which means settlement. It would just make your story more subtly authentic. If you did err on mixing up places names in England, it probably wouldn't be as bad as say a Brit with a novel in the USA naming a town (city?) Big Gulch and setting it in Maine.

The Weather

. . .

Almost without fail, a Brit will say something about the weather on meeting another Brit. "Lovely weather for ducks" is a common phrase. Yes, the UK is noted for having wet weather, however, when you compare various places in the UK with places in the USA, it's about the same. Americans from the Pacific Northwest, would feel quite at home.

During the Regency period the weather was particularly dire. Here are a few words to describe different kinds of rain that your characters may encounter though I'm sure you already use some of these in the USA: Drencher, downpour, drizzle, mizzle (misty drizzle), haar (from the sea, Scotland, N. England, misty, soft rain), lashing (down), pelting (down), sheets of rain, spitting (just beginning to rain; sometimes it turns into a shower, sometimes just lets up), sprinkling, sunshower (it's sunny, but there's a short but light shower of rain), shower, sleet (ice mixed with rain), squall (a small storm), thunderstorm, torrent/torrential rain. Rain can be soft or horizontal when windy.

If you have any Scots characters they may use smirr, smizzle (soft drizzle) and *dreich* which is sort of describes a gloomy, cloudy, not necessarily wettish day; it's pronounced dree-ch (German ch like in Bach) And though there are rainy days, it doesn't always rain all day long, or all week. So as in modern times, cricket matches can be held on village greens in between rain showers with notices that say "Rain stopped play" when players and spectators would go in for a pint or a cuppa, your Regency characters can hold an outing that might be deferred a day or two. But, as mentioned, weather was wetter and colder than normal during the whole Regency period. (A pea souper is a particularly thick fog which happened in London a few times during that period though this is more likely to be said by a lower class person than upper class.).

People

Though you may be writing predominantly in London, there would be Irish, Scots and Welsh in town, with upper class, military (many of the main generals/admirals in the Napoleonic Wars were Irish and Scots; [BTW, please don't call the Scots, Scotch which means whisky; Scottish or Scotsman or Scotswoman is fine], physicians (some of the best medical schools were in Edinburgh and Glasgow), and servants. Furthermore, because of the wars, there would be allies such as Germanic states (Austria, Saxony, Prussia, etc.; Germany didn't become a country until 1871), Russians, Portuguese and later, Spanish after 1808. There would have been a few blacks, mostly servants (not slaves). So London was as cosmopolitan then as it is today and you may want to people your story with a few characters from these groups.

Language

Most people in the US seem to think there are two accents in the UK: upper class (or Southern England/BBC) English or Cockney. I once had a girl ask me if I spoke Cockney. I said no, do you speak Bronx? Cockney comes from a very small part of London. If you do have characters who are lower class, especially outside London, look up the accents from those areas though it wouldn't be necessary to use a lot of dialect. There are many videos where you can hear the different accents.

Vulgar or what linguistics call, taboo words, differ. What is considered taboo in the USA, is not necessarily considered taboo in the UK and vice versa. However, the f-word is bad on both sides of the Pond. I was shocked when I came to the USA to hear someone refer to a friend as a "little bugger." To me that equated to homosexuality or a vulgar word for dissatisfaction. It is now more acceptable in the UK, though mildly vulgar. So if you do have any mild swearing in your novel, look up the words first, not only for their meaning and reception in the UK, but also when it was first coined.

A few things: British say half-past seven, not seven thirty; ten to eight, quarter past three. We also say "to hospital," not "to the hospital." Pants means underpants in the UK. I sometimes forget when I'm visiting with cousins in Scotland and use pants instead of trousers and my cousins always call me on it. But, pants, i.e. underpants weren't worn in the Regency period. I just wanted to point out that a man would be wearing trousers after the fashion changed from breeches.

Karen Pierotti was born in Edinburgh, but didn't spend any time there as her father was in the Royal Air Force (RAF) so they moved and lived in many places within the UK and at one time in Gibraltar, a British Territory in Spain. She worked in Lugano which is in the Italian part of Switzerland, but also spent several holidays (vacations) in various parts of Europe. She also had a lot of different secretarial jobs,

working mostly in London. This means she knows the UK quite well as she's lived in many different areas.

She writes, "I've lived in Utah for about forty years and worked at a local university for 29 years. I have a BA in English and a MA in rhetoric, and taught part-time as an instructor of first-year writing at the university. So for many years my writing was academic. I'm also a genealogist and the reason I started writing fiction was after I took a creative writing class to help make family histories more interesting. We were supposed to write a novel so I decided to write a historical novel based in Scotland though it has nothing to do with any ancestors, though genealogical research helped. It took me a long time to finish as I kept stopping and starting, but I eventually self-published Joy to My Love under my maiden name, Karen M. Edwards. "Kilconquhar Loch," a short story based on a Scottish myth, was accepted in an anthology of rewritten lesser-known fairy tales, Of Fae and Fate. My current WIP is a mystery-romance set in Gibraltar in 1810 and I hope to publish it at the end of 2020 or the beginning of 2021. Unlike everyone else, I'm a slow writer, but I plug along to the finish."

A widow of 27 years, Karen has four children and six grandchildren who live in Seattle and San Juan Island, WA, Richmond, VA, and Murray, Utah.

Check out Karen Pierotti's website, www. karenmedwards.com, where she shares various historical facts from her research, and her books as Karen M. Edwards.

RULES OF THE HEART: A FICTIONAL ILLUSTRATION

For a modern author, I couldn't resist having characters push back against the rules. If you choose to have your characters break them, make sure the reason is credible and consistent with their character. And know that those who break rules risk getting shunned by society.

To illustrate how rules in Regency England would pertain to specific situations, I had Lady Serena's governess, Miss Linsdown, tutor her in this fictional Day in the life of a Duke's daughter. I have underlined the actual rules if you just want to skim.

This is a bonus scene from *Lady Serena's Choice* I wrote expressly for *Rapid Regency*.

"Why must I always have to follow rules?" Sixteen-year-old Serena cried out in the schoolroom. Her two younger sisters were elsewhere. Miss Linsdown had requested what she characterized was a long overdue discussion for the eldest daughter of the Duke of Delaval.

The governess, looking older in her plain dress than her thirty some odd years, pressed her lips together. "My dear Lady Serena, you don't have to."

"I . . . don't?"

"No. Not if you don't care what the world thinks."

Serena walked to the window. "I don't care what the world thinks."

Her eyes followed a movement by the large barn—Sebastian Bromley leading out a horse, Papa's new purchase. The eighteen-year-old son of the head groom was dressed professionally, as was expected of the duke's more senior stable staff, in a crisp white shirt and well-fitting breeches. However, the top button of his shirt was undone, as though in a fit of impatience, he had loosened it.

"You *do* care what people would think of your family, don't you?" Miss Linsdown asked.

Serena's finger traced the windowsill, recently dusted and spotless. "Of course I do." Still, she raised her fingertips to the cool windowpane, as though she could, by this means, be with Sebastian.

One huge rule that she *could* choose to break. But she wouldn't. She'd been raised to follow rules. And that included *not* falling in love with the head groom's son.

Miss Linsdown continued. "I know most, if not all of this, would simply be a review for you, Lady Serena, but listen well, please. Morning calls are best done after noon—"

"Why are they called thus? Morning calls in the afternoon." Serena bristled. "That does not make sense."

"—for not over a half hour. You may call on your neighbors, as they are your equals or inferiors, but you must wait for an invitation from a member of the royal family. They could leave you a card to indicate their pleasure."

"Likely for that to happen. Perhaps if Prinny wished to talk horses with Papa."

"Anyone that moves to Derryshire must wait to be invited by your Papa before they can introduce themselves to the family. Although if they wish, with us being in the country, it's acceptable for them to leave a card. Or your Papa can pay a call on them, and they could return the visit. If a gentleman were making a social visit, he would ask for your Mama. If a business call, he would ask for your Papa."

"Mama is usually indisposed," Serena said, thinking of Mama and her mysterious malady that kept her laying on a chaise lounge all day.

"In that case, when you are of age or if the caller was a long-standing friend, you may accept the call in the morning room or drawing room on her behalf."

"A long-standing friend." Serena wondered about Sebastian. He was a stable boy. And a friend. She doubted highly that Miss Linsdown had him in mind.

"A lady," Miss Linsdown said, "either married or single, did not call at a man's lodging."

Serena wondered what Sebastian's lodgings were like in the stables. Did he have everything neat and tidy, or in disarray? Did he throw his shirt over the back of a worn chair, or hang it carefully on a hook? What kind of hair dressing did he use? Did he look in a little mirror to comb back his wavy brown locks?

She would never know, would she?

"Furthermore," the governess intoned, "an unengaged couple may not be alone in a room, post letters to each other, nor address each other by their Christian names. They may not travel alone in a closed horse carriage."

"Finally, something interesting," Serena muttered under her breath, seizing upon the word *horse*.

"You may drive your own carriage, but only when a groom accompanies you."

"Someone like Sebastian?" Serena asked, trying to keep her tone casual, as she looked back at the governess.

A frown formed between Miss Linsdown's pale brows. "Not Sebastian, no. Someone else . . . older perhaps."

She meant less attractive, no doubt. Less dangerous to Serena's heart.

Serena stared at the spinster governess thoughtfully. "Have you ever been in love, Miss Linsdown?"

Miss Linsdown blinked. "Have I? Heavens, whatever brought that thought to your mind?"

Serena turned back to the window and caught the reflection of her smile. "If we are to talk about carriages, we should carry out the conversation in one."

Serena almost felt bad. Getting equipped for a carriage simply to talk manners involved a lot of work. To her surprise, Miss Linsdown didn't object when Sebastian appeared to be the only one available to take them around in a carriage. Perhaps Miss Linsdown felt her company was enough to keep everything respectable.

Thank goodness she couldn't see into Serena's wayward heart. Nor could she see the secret glance Serena spared for Sebastian's broad and muscular back. When they first came out to talk to him, he gave her a piercing look, after which he was careful to not eye her directly. Even though she had willed him to.

Serena kept her frustration tucked in her heart like her hands primly folded on her lap.

Miss Linsdown didn't miss a beat. She was all about

business. "You must never drive a carriage on the open road —unless you are in the country—and certainly not in a race."

Serena's mind traveled back to that summer day two years prior, when she raced Sebastian on horseback.

When she first fell in love with him.

"You can ride or drive with a man as long as a proper chaperone—an older or married woman—is in attendance," the governess intruded in her reverie.

"Not a groom?"

"No." Miss Linsdown shook her head. "You can drive or ride without a chaperone if he is a relative or close family friend."

And here Serena was thinking she could ask Sebastian to chaperone her on a carriage ride with one of her suitors.

"And no galloping in Hyde Park." Miss Linsdown punctuated this with a censorious glance. "Except for the early mornings."

Serena sighed. "I know. Must you remind me of that indiscretion every opportune moment?"

"And you may ride sedately—

"—during the promenade hour between four thirty and seven thirty in the evening," Serena finished.

Miss Linsdown beamed, no doubt thinking that her teachings were getting through to Serena. "Precisely."

Sebastian turned his head, enabling her to see his profile. His lip twitched before facing forward. It happened so quickly Serena wondered if she had imagined it. With a flick of his wrist, he urged the horses to move on.

A pleasurable shiver prickled her neck. Serena glanced at the gardens and the sprawling grounds beyond. How much more beautiful everything suddenly seemed.

Later, sitting in front of her mirror, Serena let her maid Millie fuss over her. She wanted to look especially nice for dinner as they expected company—her friend Amelie and her parents. Though she was excited at the prospect of her friend's arrival, Serena's mind was elsewhere, thinking of a young man with meltingly brown eyes and a charming smile.

Reflected in the mirror, Miss Linsdown paced the room, her nervous energy spilling over to Serena. Back and forth, she would open her fan, then close it with a decisive thwack. Ever unswerving, she continued her lecture.

"Without being arrogant or prideful, you must keep servants and social inferiors at a proper distance. You must be civil in your interactions with servants but not casual as though they were your equal. You must not discuss private business in front of them."

The fan opened once again.

Serena watched Millie's hands work busily over her coiffure. When she was done, the maid stood back, admiring her work.

"Thank you," Serena said, looking directly into Millie's eyes. Millie beamed and curtsied.

Finally, Miss Linsdown was done for the day. It was time to go into dinner.

Serena had dressed like she was expected to. She would observe the conventions once she joined the dinner party. Her friend, Amelie, her Earl father and her mother, were coming to join them.

But first . . .

Serena walked sedately from her bedroom down the hallway and descended the stairs. No one could fault her for her graceful bearing as she reached the front door and stepped out into the deepening twilight.

Just as she had hoped, Sebastian was walking a horse the direction of the barn.

He stopped in his steps. She could barely make out his figure in the dusk. But she knew it was him. "Good evening," he greeted her from across the grounds.

She would have to hurry. Someone would notice her absence if she were gone for too long. Picking up her skirts, she walked toward him then stopped. The horse stood between them.

"How is he coming along?" she asked of Papa's new horse.

"Very well."

She reached up and trailed her fingers along the gelding's mane, leaning close against his warmth and hiding her face from Sebastian. She needed to collect her thoughts so she could speak coherently. In his presence, her mouth turned dry.

Sebastian reached up too, his hand traveling the contour of the horse's mane. With fascination, she watched as his fingers grazed and then covered hers, sending sparks zinging her skin up and down her arm.

She felt dizzy. Out of breath.

Pulling back, but not too quickly, she didn't dare look into his eyes. "Thank you for the carriage ride today," she whispered.

He didn't answer right away. She wondered if he'd heard her. As moments ticked by, her curiosity got the best of her. She raised her eyes to his and was caught in the heat of his gaze. Her bosom burned with longing.

"Anytime, my lady." His voice had deepened as a man's even more so this season.

Her heart hammering, she backed away and then turned back to the grand house. Back to the dinner party. Back to her life of rules.

As she entered the house, she closed the door and leaned momentarily against the wall. Her eyes fluttered shut as she steadied her breath, and then she glanced down at her hand.

She could still feel the imprint of his touch.

Raising her knuckles to her lips, she kissed them with a delicious shiver and smiled.

Want to read more of Sebastian and Serena's story? Check out *Lady Serena's Choice on Amazon.*

31

Q&AS

I HAD the pleasure of interviewing several Regency romance authors for my weekly Author Q&A's on my blog in 2019 and 2020. The following two Q&A's give a candid, inspiring snapshot of their journey as a Regency romance author. Enjoy!

Q&A: Remarkable Romances with Josi Kilpack

Josi Kilpack is the award-winning author of historical and contemporary romances, as well as culinary mysteries. She will talk about how her remarkably successful culinary mystery series evolved, how she prepared to write her Regency romances, and what she's doing to fill her creative well. Date of Interview: May 1, 2020

. . .

Q. Hi Josi! Thanks for chatting with me today.

A. Thank YOU for inviting me to chat.

Q. For the benefit of our readers. I wanted to say I've known you for a while, first through Storymakers. I think it has been about a decade. So we were just babies then.

A. Hahaha. No kidding. And we had babies. All of mine are all grown up now. Crazy.

Q. Yes; crazy! I'll come right out and say, that's what made me think to chat you up...you said you are applying to be a real estate agent because your kids are grown. Did I sum that up right?

A. Yep, I've finished the course and take the test next week. As my kids have grown up and become more independent, my involvement with things like activities and school have been less and less. I've found that being home all the time, and often by myself, does not give me the content I need to be creative. So, without kids at home I'm starting a new career that is meant to stretch my brain and give me that interaction essential to creativity. At least for me. I know lots of people who can be full time writers, but I have realized I'm not one of them.

Q. Wow! That is an interesting philosophy. Can you explain more about that last sentence, because um, I will be honest...if I had as much success as you I could see myself doing that to eternity.

A. I think creativity comes through imagination and consumption. Consumption comes from what fills the wells of the imagination. For instance, could I have ever imagined a dragon if I hadn't seen someone else's idea of what a dragon is. I think some people can do that, but it doesn't work for me. I draw from conversation and interactions with people, watching, observing, and imagining a different conclusion to a conversation. So, in this last year as my oldest has been a super busy senior in high school and I'm not helping out with school fundraisers or sitting on the sidelines for soccer games, my "interaction" has become more and more limited. We moved from a community we had lived in for 20 years and so I didn't have the connections I had come to take for granted. But I had ALL this time! The writing has been harder forever and though it's not only because I am my own company most of the time, I have realized that's part of it. My daughter will go to college in August and I need to "get a life." so to speak.

One of my favorite quotes is "That which takes me from my writing gives me something to write about." That has proven very true for me.

Q. Like filling your creative well. That is so true! And I can relate so much, now that my kids are all in college or missions. How did you choose to pivot into a new career in real estate? And what does it take to prepare for it? How long was the course?

A. I own and manage a few properties, my ex-husband loved buying and selling real estate, so I had a basis of how it worked. I have a couple of friends who are also RE agents and I've watched how they have created a career for themselves. I asked A LOT of questions and then, at the urging of another friend who was getting her license, signed up for the course. In Utah there are online courses available. I started on January 13 and finished on April 13. The testing centers have been closed but I was able to schedule my test on May 6th. I'm excited and super nervous. But I need to do something and this feels right to me. Let's hope I'm right!

Q. That is fantastic. Good for you, and I am sure you will do great. It couldn't have come at a better time.

Everyone is online anyway! Well, I can honestly say that you are an author whom I have always looked up to. Not just because you write beautiful books, but because you have always been so kind and helpful to other authors like me. And your philosophy about not defining yourself just on your writing speaks volumes about how grounded you are. Let's step back for a minute and can you tell me how you got started in publishing?

A. A million years ago—or, I guess, 21+ years ago—I was on bedrest with a pregnancy. I was fighting depression and sheer boredom and started writing a story inspired by too much Lifetime Television for women and contemporary LDS fiction, which was a relatively new genre at the time. My intention was to have something fun to do, but it turned into a full length book by the time my baby was 6 weeks old. It was fun enough that I wanted to keep doing it, but I had an awful lot to learn. I paid for the publication of that first book through a small publishers and though it did not do well, I wanted this whole story-writing-thing to be a part of my life. I started attending writing conferences, meeting other writers, reading critically, and I kept writing. I had a lot to learn, I still do, but it has become a powerful and important part of my life. I can't imagine who I would be without it. I've met the best people through my writing, including you. You were in one of my "Bootcamp" groups back then. I'm so glad you're still in the writing world.

Q. Wow, great memory. You are so right! It was at boot-camp! And you were very encouraging so here I am years later, following your advice not to quit. What would you say was your breakthrough book/s? Was it your culinary series or something else?

A. Definitely *Lemon Tart*, the first book in my Sadie Hoffmiller culinary mystery series. It outsold my prior books by almost double and was the start of a series that came in 6 month increments. I had to write twice as fast but the readers loves Sadie and it allowed me to write 12 books in that series. It was a huge turning point for my writing career.

Q. You have a mouthwatering mystery series featuring an endearing heroine. It is one of my favorite genres, and as a foodie, I would love to know how that series got produced. For instance...how far in advance did you plan the entire series? How did you come up with the recipes?

A. When I submitted *Lemon Tart* it was a standalone book without recipes. They suggested I include recipes for some of the things Sadie (then named Betty) made during the story–hence it became a culinary mystery. During that part of the process I mentioned to them I had an idea for the same character in a second book set in England. They agreed to a three book series at which point I put out a request on my blog for readers who would be willing to help me develop the recipes. The first eight people to respond became "Sadie's Test Kitchen" and they helped with all the books in the series. When English Trifle was well received, we decided to go to five books, then seven, ten and finally twelve. I was the one who put a stop to the series–I was running out of ways to kill people and reasons why. I wanted the books to feel different from each other and not be the same plot told over and over again with different names and places.

The test kitchen would give me recipe ideas and then make all the recipes to make sure they worked in other people's kitchens and were "book" worthy.

Q. The Test Kitchen sounds fun and brilliant. "Running out of ways to kill people and reasons why." LOL What inspired you to write a mystery?

A. I wrote the first chapter for a blog contest sponsored by Jeff Savage who was writing a mystery novel at the time. I was between projects, considering trying to get into the national market, and ready for a challenge. I had never written a mystery or a non-LDS character before. I didn't win the contest (though I got 2nd place) but all the work I had put in to figuring out how to write that first chapter made me want to keep writing. I plucked away at that book for another two years, in between my LDS-character novels, and when it was done asked Deseret Book for a release of contract that would allow me to shop it nationally. They said to send it in so they could properly reject it and free me up to pursue other publication, and then loved it. They were looking for non-LDS but clean fiction and Sadie fit the bill.

Q. Nice! What did you learn about story and romance arcs in a series? How did you develop side characters? What did your readers keep clamoring for more?

A. I learned that arcs in a series are really tricky. There are story arcs in each book, but also series arcs that stretch over multiple books. Romance is especially tricky because if they get together too quickly, then you lose some of the tension of your story. I learned this as I went, since I didn't plan the series in advance. Sadie had to grow but she couldn't grow so much that she was unrecognizable to the reader in the next book. Side characters were specifically developed in regard to what Sadie and the story needed from them. My readers just wanted more of all of it—recipes, Sadie's antics, new places. The readers are amazing and they are the reason the series went on as long as it did. Series typically sell well at first but decrease by each book. This is true for Sadie as well, except by about book 4 the sales stayed the same and all the books went up when a new book came out. It was remarkable.

Q. Yes it was. Apart from your culinary mysteries and LDS fiction, you also write Regency romances. In all, your books number over 30 according to your Zon bio. Regency has a tender spot in my heart. When I was a brand new mom some 20-years ago, escaping between their pages was something I enjoyed. I am pretty sure I checked out all the Regencies I could get my hands on. How did you get into Regencies?

A. The exact same way! That's amazing, Jewel. I was a new mom with no money or time for hobbies, but I could read. I would go to my local library (we lived in Salt Lake then so we had their amazing county library system) and check out the Zebra and Silhouette regencies. When I did have time to indulge, I read those books. Hundreds of them those first few years until I was too busy to read that way anymore. The first story I ever wrote was a Regency specifically to show off what I had learned about the time period. I never had any plans to publish it, and it's pure garbage, but that was my first story. A few years later I started writing what would become my first published book.

I've only written seven regencies, and three historical.

Q. I started to read one of your stories yesterday. It was about Dina...Colladina. I thought it was in my Kindle but I can't seem to find it. Remind me the title...?

A. That's one of my short stories done through Timeless Romance Anthologies, *To Love a Governess*. There are three in that particular Anthology and that one is titled '*Til the Seas Gang Dry*.

Q. Yes, that is it! There was a poignancy to their love story. She didn't seem complete without him and vice versa. I was drawn into the story from that very first sentence.

Something like she could tell it was him. (I will have to look it up exactly unless you know it by heart.)

A. She's outside with the girl she's a governess for and he comes to find her–after several years apart–and she knows it's him without looking. For no particular reason than that she just knows. I'm so glad you liked it.

Q. Yes. I loved that your characters seemed to have...a certain gravity. How much would you say of yourself and your life experiences make it into your books?

A. I'm not really sure. I would say I'm a person who has a lot of "feelings" so I can tap into all the things a character needs—love, desire, loneliness, fear–and there are aspects of a lot of the characters I can relate to, but even if they start with a situation I had in my life, it always evolves through the course of the story into something else. So, I know that my life experience contributes, but I feel like it mashes together and grinds through the creative process enough that it becomes unrecognizable.

Q. Makes sense. It's personal and yet universal. When you hit that sweet spot, it can certainly be gold. What would you advice an aspiring Regency author? Between all that research and manners and language, it seems almost easier not to try.

A. I'm a lazy researcher, it is not my favorite part of the process. I'm going to really unimpress people, so hang in there—watch movies. I find movies are a much easier way of figuring out the culture and the speech patterns. Take lots of notes–like writing out the response, identifying the slang, stuff like that. Read Georgette Heyer–she's my favorite for getting the right "feel." or better yet, listen to her books so you hear the accent. Then write your story using what you think you know, but make notes to yourself about stuff you need to research. I use ## because it's easy to search in a document. On days when the writing isn't working, or when the book is finished, I go research those specific details. For instance I'm writing about the wife of a knight and don't know how she be introduced at a party I'll make my best guess then put in a ## and then at some point I'll google "how is the wife of a knight addressed in public" and amend my scene accordingly. Choose sites that feel legit, like those written by other regency writers or via Debretts. And expect you'll get some things wrong and some reader will say you're a hack and admit that you're a storyteller, not a historian, and go on with your life.

Most readers just want a great story and if you can get enough facts right to keep them from being pulled out of the story, you're in good shape. If you can't find a specific help then vague it out. Instead of saying "Sir and Lady Bufflepuff," the footman announced, causing heads to turn in their direction. You say, "Upon their announcement, heads turned in their direction." Story first, people, that's my motto.

Q. Love that advice! I can't believe our time is up, but alas it is. Thanks so much for chatting with me. I enjoyed catching up with you and wish you the best with your exam next week, and your new leaf in life.

A. Thank you, Jewel, this is the best format I've ever done for an interview. You are wonderful and I'm glad you're still writing. Thanks so much.

Check out Josi Kilpack's books on Amazon and her website, www.josikilpack.com.

∽

Q&A : Writing Fun Books with Maggie Dallen

Maggie Dallen is the bestselling author of sweet romance in multiple genres, including Young Adult, Regency, and contemporary adult. She will chat about how she writes in multiple genres, how that helped her find her voice, and how she gets her fun book ideas. Date of interview: October 3, 2020

Q. How is your Friday shaping up? (Yay Friday!!)

A. So far so good, thanks! It's been a big writing week for me so I'm very much looking forward to a brain break this weekend!

Q. Goodness. Give me a sec. I looked out the window and what did I see?

A. Whaaat? Are they yours?

Q. . . . cows that do not belong to me!

A. Lol. Oh dear. They don't look happy.

Q. Luckily they left my yard before they ate my geraniums and are now mosying down the road. I called dispatch. Okay... where was I...?

A. Haha! where do you live?

Q. I live in Utah, in a city about 40 miles west of Salt Lake City. Glad your Friday is going great, ha! Tell me about your writing week. What did it look like?

A. Well, I typically only work on two books at a time but this week I have three on my plate, so my head is just spinning right now. LOL I usually try to write around 5K words 5 days a week—that's the pace I've found works best for me while still allowing me to stay on top of marketing and editing, etc. But this week will be more like a 30-35K week when all is said and done.

Q. Three! Whoa. Are they in different genres? (And thanks for making time for me today. I am sure you will be recharged by this–I hope!)

A. Yes, I was looking forward to this break! They are each in different genres: a sweet historical Christmas novella, a sweet small-town contemporary, and a YA romance.

I typically know better than to juggle three at once but my writing calendar got all shifted around so I'm trying to make it work.

Q. That is amazing. Do you have pre-orders due soon or something?

A. Yeah, I'm shifting my calendar around to accommo-date editors' schedules and group projects. After this week I should be back on track!

Q. FYI, I have watched all your videos on the recent Writing Gals conference, and I truly enjoyed them and learned a lot.

A. Oh thanks!

Q. I know if I were to pick your brain it would be like a library of books worth, so I will do my best to dial into specific things.

A. Hahaha, hit me! I love talking about writing and publishing more than anything so I'm here for it.

Q. In your best Cliff notes version, how did you get from point A (where you started writing) to now where you are publishing wildly successfully in multiple genres? That is probably not a fair question.

Tell me about your jobs along the way. I am speaking as a former journalist myself.

A. Cliff Notes, huh? Okay, I'll try!

Q. Write as long as you want!

A. Let's see, I finished my first book way back in 2002. (I'd started many but that was the first full-length I actually finished.) Back in 2002 self-pub wasn't a thing so I went the trad pub route and over the next....oh, 15 years or so, had a whole lot of close calls, heartbreaking misses, and more rejection letters than I could ever count. I never stopped writing, though! In that time I held down a crazy amount of day jobs and freelance gigs to pay the bills, including but not limited to executive assistant, bartender, freelance editor, proofreader, news editor, journalist, and ghostwriter.

I first dipped my toes in self-pub in 2015 when I also got my first deal with a publisher. In 2016 I discovered two things: 20booksto50K® (and some other indie groups) and that I really didn't like the trad route!

Q. Yes, that's it. I knew you had been down the writing path. The bartending sounds interesting.

A. When I had my baby at the end of 2018 my husband and I had a major decision to make. Whether I was going back to my day job or stay home. I won't bore you with all the details there but we eventually decided that I'd stay home for the first two years and try to make a go of the writing career. It was PRESSURE! Not from my husband (he's so wonderfully supportive) but I put a ton of pressure on myself. In my mind, this was my last chance. (I have a tendency for melodrama!) But in all honesty, I'd been writing steadily for close to 20 years with zero to show for it financially and we now had a mouth to feed and a house to buy and...you know. Adult stuff.

So, yeah....my Cliff Notes version is getting way too long. In 2018 I decided to take everything I'd been learning from these FB groups and put it into action. And...it worked!

Q. Yeah, I hear you on adulting. You are doing great. It's the Cliff notes chat version. Tell me the top three things that you put into action?

A. Writing to market and rapid releasing were the biggies.

Q. How did you decide what market to write to? And what genre was that? What kinds of books?

A. I didn't. LOL When I first started self-pub I was writing *everything*. Seriously. Everything. Like, steamy romcoms and steampunk fantasies and sweet small-town and...it was a mess.

Q. I know someone who did / does that. Speaking for a friend.

A. But I honestly wasn't sure what to cut out of the mix because writing in multiple genres makes me happy! But, I did realize that I had to focus. To help me decide where to focus, I took my favorite genres and gave them each a fair shot.

Q. I really enjoyed your writing in multiple genres video and why doing so makes you happy. They make me happy too. Which were your faves?

A. The ones that ended up making the cut were sweet YA, sweet adult small-town, and sweet historical. As you can see, I finally found *some* focus, at least. I discovered pretty quickly that I tend to write sweet and that's where my readers were. I'm so glad I didn't just pick the one where I had the most books out because I never would have found the great niche I've discovered in the sweet YA (Young Adult) world.

Q. Tell me what kind of learning curve you did for YA. Because it seems intimidating though all of us were youth at one time.

You know, with YA, I feel like I had just some really

good luck. I happened to hit it out of the park with one of my first attempts at YA contemporary romance and a lot of that was luck. It was one of those great moments where I hit upon a good trope, good cover, and a good premise in a hungry market. That success definitely included a lot of luck and good timing. The part that I feel like I can take credit for is how I leapt on that luck! I ended up turning that one successful book into a successful six-book series and used the momentum from a lucky break to really establish myself with the YA crowd.

Q. Nice! Which book was that?

A. *Out of His League.*

Q. * Looking it up right now * Whoa. I am scrolling for miles (you have a lot of books!) and I still can't find it...

A. That was one of my earliest self-pub books, my second YA.

Q. Found it. Briarwood High series, correct?

A. Ha ha yes!

Q. So how did you come up with the concept for this book?

A. This cover was a premade cover by Shari Ryan and I took one look at it and was inspired to write a book about a tomboy who tries to start over as a girlie girl. This was the first (but definitely *not* the last) time I wrote a book based on a cover.

Q. Yes! I totally can relate. Sometimes it is much easier to write to a cover than vice versa.

Q. How many words was it more or less? On average how long are your YA books?

A. My YA books are 45-55K on average. I have a series of novellas releasing right now which are around 30K.

Q. Was it semi-autobiographical? You seem to write a lot of sports romances.

A. NO! Not at all. I love sports romances but was never into sports, which is sometimes (embarrassingly) glaringly obvious to readers. Ha!

Q. Seriously? That is surprising. I have noticed your Regency romances recently since I am jumping into the genre myself. Lovely and *fun* covers. They have a YA vibe. I mean, one of your series is about a finishing school, right?

A. Yes! I'm working on the last book of that series right now. With writing in multiple genres, I've tried to find this balance between my brand and being to market. By that I mean, I want people to see my books and know they're written by me...but also be very clear what genre they're picking up. Yes, I try to keep a lighthearted, fluffy, romcom vibe across the board!

Q. I read a sample of one of your Regencies, and I definitely get the rom-com vibe. I mean, the cover and title set it up for it. Was that a conscious decision on your part?

A. Yes! You nailed it with that question.

Q. I definitely think it fits your brand. Everything about you, how you convey yourself on a webinar, your covers, etc. Good job!

A. Thanks! I joke with my friends that my tagline should read: You will never cry reading my books.

Q. LOL How did you research your Regencies? How did you segue from your contemporary stuff to Regency? Because again, that's a hard mental block to overcome. At least it was for me. PS Of course, it may have been helpful you were already doing steampunk.

A. Yeah, funny story about that. That steampunk book actually started off as my first attempt at regency romance. I got so overwhelmed with fears about historical accuracy that on page three I added an airship and declared it steampunk. *That* was how scared I used to be of messing up historical accuracy.

Q. I just laughed out loud. I totally understand that fear. Hey, I think an airship makes steampunk. No quarrel with me there.

A. Yeah, once I realized that with steampunk I could create my own rules, I was into it! I was like "how would she have received word so quickly?" An AIRSHIP! Done and done. That's the beauty of fantastical worlds.

Q. No kidding! That is great. How did you transition to Regency then? You make me think Regency is gowns without the airships.

A. Hahaha! I was reading historical romances more than any other for many years, and finally I took the plunge. (After the steampunk endeavor.) I tried again, and this time I did all the research. And then I tried again. The first one I actually published was maybe the fourth novella I'd written in that genre.

Q. How do you write in multiple genres where the language might be somewhat or starkly different? Like contemporary to Regency in the same week?

A. It took me a while to get a handle on historical. Not just the historical accuracy, but my voice. I'm still working on that. My first series that I published...it feels so slow and clunky to me when I go back and read it now.

Q. Yeah, that makes sense. I am sure you get more confident of your voice as you keep writing in that genre.

A. I'm working to try and take what makes my contemporaries fun and lighthearted and try and translate that into my historical voice. I think I am making progress but the key, for me, is to just keep writing.

A. I feel like progress in writing isn't as linear as any of us would like. There are going to be leaps forward and then steps back, right?

Q. Yup! I need to know why you are so funny. There's prob a funny story behind that.

A. You think I'm funny??

Q. It's your delivery.

A. Ha! Oh, that's good to know.

Q. I will just have to refer everyone to the Writing Gals Conference to hear more of your brilliant advice because we are out of time (I was going to say sadly but it doesn't fit your brand, ha ha).

So I will wrap up with a question that goes back to how I first heard of you. You used to make book trailers. And they were brilliant. Watching three-second trailers made me want to write all your sweet book ideas. How do you come up with yours?

A. Oh thanks! I hope to get back to the video ads. It got put on hold thanks to COVID but that's my favorite pastime. As for how I get my ideas...I have no idea. LOL. Honestly, I'm a little afraid to overthink it in case I mess with whatever magic brings about new ideas! Some books have come about because of premade book covers, others started with an opening line and then took on a life of its own from there. (I can tell you the first line, actually: "It was a butt dialing disaster of epic proportions.") Some come about as I'm writing (my secondary characters are LOUD and they demand stories.) The other day I was watching The Wizard of Oz with my son and had to pull out a notepad and jot down notes because the wicked witch gave me an idea... So yeah, they come from all over!

Q. That is awesome, like you. I wish we had more time. I will have to do another Q&A with you someday between deadlines (ha ha), just focusing on another genre. Thanks so much Maggie for your time. Good luck with all the words this week; you will rock them I am sure.

A. Thanks so much for chatting...that was fun.

You can find out more about Maggie Dallen's books on her Amazon page and on Facebook (MaggieDallenAuthor)

32

PARTING WORDS

I HOPE that you have found this book helpful. Refer back to it for ideas and encouragement as you write all your lovely Regency romances!

The beauty of this time period's popularity is, there are so many resources available to us authors. Once you get your feet under you, spread your wings and explore the many other aspects of this fascinating time in history.

Thank you for reading *Rapid Regency*!

Honest reviews would be appreciated. Check out the rest of my Rapid Release series for authors. Read my rapid release experiments and updates on my Facebook page (Jewel Allen) and subscribe to my newsletter (www.jewelallen.com/subscribe).

Best of luck to you on your own writing adventure!

33

———————

RESOURCES

THIS IS by no means an exhaustive list of resources, but it will get you started. They are ones I personally used in my research or have been recommended to me. It is tempting to get anything and everything related to the period. My suggestion is to start with a few good sources, and then expand your library and reading as your time, money and interest allow.

Books

Adkins, Roy & Lesley. *Jane Austen's England*

Kloester, Jennifer *Georgette Heyer's Regency World*

Pool, Daniel. *What Jane Austen Ate and Charles Dickens*

Knew: From Fox Hunting to Whist—the Facts of Daily Life in Nineteenth-Century England.

Uglow, Jenny. *In These Times* - Great resource for daily life of ordinary people during Georgian / Regency England.

Websites / Blogs

Britannica
  Donna Hatch
  Historical Hussies
  Jane Austen's World
  Karen Pierotti
  Kristen Koster – She has a great resources link.
  Nicola Cornick
  Random Bits Of Fascination – Written by Maria Grace, who has a series of Regency reference books (and novels) on Amazon.
  Regina Jeffers
  Second Battalion 95th Rifles
  Shannon Donnelly
  The Beau Monde
  Vanessa Riley
  Wikipedia
  Word Wenches

Facebook Groups for Sweet Regency Authors

•   •   •

Historymakers

Sweet Historical Romance Newsletter Swap Group